INFORMATION TRADING

how information influences the health policy process

Marion Ein Lewin and Elise Lipoff, *Editors*

A Project of
The Robert Wood Johnson Health Policy Fellowships Program
at the
Institute of Medicine

Sponsored by The Robert Wood Johnson Foundation

NATIONAL ACADEMY PRESS
Washington, D.C. 1997

NATIONAL ACADEMY PRESS • 2101 Constitution Avenue, N.W. • Washington, DC 40218

NOTICE: This publication is based on a series of papers commissioned for the Annual Alumni Gathering of the Robert Wood Johnson Health Policy Fellows held on October 12–13, 1996. The views expressed are those of the authors and do not necessarily reflect those of the Institute of Medicine.

The Office of Health Policy Programs and Fellowships at the Institute of Medicine, National Academy of Sciences, is the national program office for the Robert Wood Johnson (RWJ) Health Policy Fellowships Program, and in this capacity, provides overall direction and runs the day-to-day operations for the program. The RWJ Health Policy Fellowships Program is funded by The Robert Wood Johnson Foundation. For more information about the Fellowships Program, visit its home page at **http://www2.nas.edu/rwj.**

The Institute of Medicine was chartered in 1970 by the National Academy of Sciences to enlist distinguished members of the appropriate professions in the examination of policy matters pertaining to the health of the public. In this, the Institute acts under both the Academy's 1863 congressional charter responsibility to be an adviser to the federal government and its own initiative in identifying issues of medical care, research, and education. Dr. Kenneth I. Shine is president of the Institute of Medicine.

For more information about the Institute of Medicine, visit the IOM home page at **http://www.nas.edu/iom.**

Support for this project was provided by the The Robert Wood Johnson Foundation. The opinions expressed in this publication are those of the authors and do not necessarily reflect the views of the sponsor.

International Standard Book Number 0-309-05793-0

Additional copies of this publication are available for sale from the National Academy Press, 2101 Constitution Avenue, N.W., Box 285, Washington, DC 20055; call (800) 624-6242 or (202) 334-3313 (in the Washington metropolitan area), or visit the NAP's on-line bookstore at **http://www.nap.edu.**

Printed in the United States of America

Acknowledgments

This book was truly a team effort, and it reflects the ideas and contributions of many different people. The use of information to shape and influence public policy has always been a subject of compelling interest, particularly in Washington, D.C., where information and information trading is the business, if not passion, of many groups and individuals. Shortly after the Robert Wood Johnson (RWJ) Health Policy Fellows come to town each year to begin their orientation they become aware of the importance and challenges of developing the information and the message that may hold the key for the eventual success or failure of a policy or position. Thus, it is fair to say, that this book was partially inspired by all of the Washington-based policy experts who graciously meet with the Fellows year after year and educate them on the content and process of health policy formulation.

Special thanks go to Wendy Young and the other members of the 1995–1996 cohort who took major responsibility for developing the project. Deep appreciation is extended to all the contributors to this book. They took their assignments very seriously and also welcomed comments and suggestions on first, second, and sometimes third drafts, even if it meant another round of thinking and writing.

Drafts of these papers were the focus of discussion and additional commentary at 1996 Alumni Day and at a breakout session at the 1996 Annual Meeting of the Institute of Medicine. Former Fellows Robert Crittenden, Jean Paul Gagnon, Nancy Gary, Myron Genel, Barbara Langner, and Marie Michnich also deserve special thanks for their helpful review and discussion of the papers at Alumni Day.

With great appreciation, we thank the RWJ Health Policy Fellowships Program Advisory Board and its chair, Sheila Ryan, for encouraging us to do this project and for providing us with sound advice. We also thank Mike Hash, Janet Kline, and Janet Shikles, who generously contributed their respected expertise and balanced views by allowing us to "reality-test" some of the ideas in this book with them.

Great gratitude goes to a number of people at the IOM who contributed to the successful completion of this project in substantive ways. They include Clyde Behney, Nancy Diener, Mike Edington, Karen Hein, Linda Humphrey, Valerie Tate Jopeck, Justine Lang, and Kenneth Shine. Deep appreciation goes to Michael Hayes for his fine and thoughtful editing of the volume.

Last, but not least, our special thanks go to all those who work with us at The Robert Wood Johnson Foundation, for allowing the Fellowships Program the opportunity to develop this special project and for having the confidence in us to let us bring it to fruition.

Marion Ein Lewin and Elise Lipoff

Contents

INFORMATION TRADING

Foreword and Introduction

Marion Ein Lewin

The Robert Wood Johnson (RWJ) Health Policy Fellowships program, established in 1973, is designed to develop the capacities of outstanding midcareer health professionals in academic and community-based settings to gain an understanding of the health policy process and to assume leadership roles in health policy and management. Each year six Fellows are selected on a competitive basis and leave their academic settings and practice responsibilities to spend a year in the nation's capital. A 3-month orientation program is followed by a 9-month working assignment in a congressional office or in the executive branch. The Fellowships program, which is sponsored by The Robert Wood Johnson Foundation, is directed and administered by the Institute of Medicine of the National Academy of Sciences. At this writing 139 Fellows have gone through the program.

During the life of the program, virtually all the major health care issues that revolve around the triad of access, costs, and quality have come to the forefront of the nation's attention and have been discussed and debated from different policy and political perspectives depending on the year, the party in power, the health care environment, and the social and economic climate. It could be said, however, that the years 1992 to 1994, and the battle for passage of national health care reform represented an historical and unique opportunity to observe both the highs and the lows of public policy formulation. No matter what side of the issues one was positioned, the years of the Clinton health plan debate provided invaluable lessons on how things get accomplished or fall apart in a political environment around issues of major change—in this case, national health care reform.

For the RWJ Health Policy Fellows, one of the seminal lessons learned from the rise and fall of the Clinton Health Security Act (Clinton HSA) focused on how information is produced, packaged, used, and disseminated to color or position a particular issue and to affect the final outcome—in both positive and negative ways. Although this area may be old hat to Madison Avenue and the media, the use of information by key stakeholders to both shape and shake public perception and opinion was an illuminating if not transforming experience for policymakers and health policy researchers traditionally operating outside the hothouse of the Washington political scene. Symbolized perhaps most startlingly by the now-famous Harry and Louise ads developed by the insurance industry, the 1992 to 1994 policy and political season marked a uniquely rich opportunity to learn about information and information trading as critical drivers in the ultimate success or failure of a legislative initiative.

It was with this in mind that a group of RWJ Health Policy Fellows decided that it might be useful to develop a number of case studies focused on major national or state health care initiatives and to look more closely at how information is used and conveyed and to what degree it influences the outcome. The case studies selected and presented in this volume—the adoption of the successful Japanese just-in-time (JIT) manufacturing strategy to information development and trading on Capitol Hill; funding of graduate medical education (GME) as proposed in the Clinton HSA; the campaign for statewide health care reform in Missouri; the development of New York State legislation phasing out the state's hospital rate-setting system with a more market-oriented approach for funding GME and other public goods such as care for the uninsured; the recent congressional debate over reauthorization of the National Institutes of

Health (NIH); legislative efforts in the 104th U.S. Congress to regulate the use of genetic information, particularly as it pertains to insurance discrimination; and overtures in the Congress to reform Medicare payments to participating health maintenance organization (HMO) risk contractors—mark initiatives and subject areas in which the authors as current or former Fellows had an opportunity to observe firsthand how information is used to affect policy and outcomes.

Although each of the papers provides different insights and describes the different valuable lessons that the Fellows learned, certain themes resonate throughout the volume. They include the following:

• The explosion in recent years in the amount and sources of information around health care issues. The sheer volume of materials that crosses a legislator's or a staffer's desk during a typical work week is overwhelming. At the same time government at all levels is downsizing, with significant reductions in the number of staff responsible for increasingly larger workloads. The result is that staff have less and less time to devote to gaining a full understanding of a policy issue or a legislative initiative.

• To be effective, information must respond to the needs of increasingly distracted and time-pressed legislators and staff, posing special challenges for educating members on complex and technical issues. Formal testimony at congressional hearings is now, in most cases, limited to 5 minutes. In responding to the new reality, leading think tanks, research groups, and foundations are perfecting the art of producing "one-pagers," clear, concise summaries and findings of larger studies.

• In an environment of information overflow, lawmakers are prone to rely on trusted consultants, lobbyists, or brokers to help them identify aspects of proposed legislation with which the elected official wants to identify and to package and shape relevant information most supportive of the member's position and politics. Often such a politicized and fragmented focus can confuse or distort, rather than illuminate, the important underlying issue that needs to be addressed.

• As policy formulation at every level has become more budget-driven, for information to be considered useful it must include the costs and budget implications of the policy or program being advanced. The ability to provide timely, reliable, and credible cost estimates related to a particular legislative proposal or position is considered a valuable commodity.

• There has been a significant compression of time in which action on major issues takes place in Congress, a consequence in part of the increasing politicization of policymaking in Washington (as well as in the states) and the never-ending preoccupation with winning the next election. As one of the writers in this volume suggests, over the past two decades, the restructuring of congressional committees and increasing ease of travel between home districts and the Capitol have erased any earlier clear distinction between campaigning and policymaking activities. Surveys and polls indicate again and again that the voting public has a short attention span when it comes to most policy issues and political debates. Increasingly, leaders of both parties are timing action on major pieces of legislation—particularly legislation in which voters have a high level of interest—closer to the start of election campaigns.

• Although information is critical, more often than not it is not the decisive element in determining legislation in a political environment. Instead, the importance of timing, leadership, and identifying the right moment for bringing key stakeholders to the table ready "to deal" are often the make-or-break factors.

• On Capitol Hill, the use of a dramatic anecdote or packaging of a message around a personal-interest story is a time-tested vehicle for garnering public attention more quickly and memorably than the use of more comprehensive and broadly represented information.

• It is essential to understand the political, policy, and economic environments in which a particular issue is being raised, debated, and resolved.

• The democratic process and our system of checks and balances are designed to slow action on proposals of significant change. Even for a combination of a good idea and effective information it may take several years of coalition and public support building before there is a reasonable chance of passing a piece of legislation.

• This country is witnessing a democratization of leadership and decision-making, with important implications for Congress and information trading. As citizens have become increasingly cynical and impatient with government and bureaucracy, grassroots movements and legislation by referendum have become important levers for legislative action around important issues. In Congress the seniority system and all-powerful committee chairs have virtually disappeared. Key information is no longer primarily the purview of an exclusive group of leaders or professionals. Cyberspace and the internet are also contributing in major ways to the democratization of information and information trading.

Each of the seven papers in this volume expands upon and illuminates some of the themes listed above. "The Market for Information in Health Policy: Using the 'Just-in-Time' Strategy," by Wendy Young, describes how Congress, operating in an increasingly competitive and partisan environment is adopting the much heralded Japanese just-in-time manufacturing strategy for information development on Capitol Hill. The oversupply of information has exceeded the need for information at any given time and has created a reliance on JIT strategies to sort and retrieve only the information needed at the moment. Policymakers use the JIT approach to gain a competitive edge to influence policy proposals and political agendas. The paper offers interesting perspectives on how policymaking in Congress is acquiring more marketing characteristics and how individual members have identified their own fleet of consultants to advise them on media, strategy, polling, and direct mail, in many cases replacing the political party organization's traditional role. The author expresses concern that the popularity of JIT information sources may be reinforcing the shift toward privatization and downsizing, with the potential for eroding the federal capacity for conducting effective and objective evaluations of its policies.

Oliver Fein's paper, "Funding Graduate Medical Education in the Year of Health Care Reform: A Case Study of a Health Issue on Capitol Hill," traces the evolution of the 1994 GME debate in the U.S. Senate. The paper provides an informative, hands-on glimpse of health policy formulation around high-stakes issues such as proposals to establish physician workforce policies, reduce the overall number of residency training positions, redirect GME dollars from teaching hospitals to other training sites, and reduce the large variations in GME payments across institutions and regions. The paper contends that whereas the control and targeting of key information by the Clinton administration and valuable data provided by expert panels and commissions represented major forces in shaping the legislation, when it came to final action or inaction, they paled in significance to the power and influence of well-armed and sophisticated interest groups.

Dr. Fein points out that although health care reform and, with it, the GME provisions, failed to pass the Senate, the issue has remained vibrant and Congress benefited from a rich learning experience. According to the author, then majority leader Senator George Mitchell told his staff that if health reform did not pass in 1994, one consequence would be that Congress would be armed with how to make future cuts in Medicare and Medicaid. Medicare GME funding continues to be on the cutting table in the 105th Congress and may in the end fare less well than in that historical period when health care reform was addressed.

Robert Frank and Coleen Kivlahan provide a thorough assessment of a state health reform initiative in their paper, "The Use of Information and Misinformation in a State Health Reform Initiative." In Missouri as well as in most other states, the legislative process and the systems supporting the development of legislation differ from those in the U.S. Congress. State legislative sessions tend to be very short compared to those of the U.S. Congress, and part-time legislators frequently combine their roles as legislators with many other activities. Part-time legislators rarely have the time or ability to develop expertise in an area unless it is related to their occupation.

According to the authors, health care reform proposals are frequently hampered, among other things, by the lack of available state-specific data, a deficiency often exploited by powerful interest groups interested in maintaining the status quo. The authors attest that national data and trends may not be adequate evidence to force major change at the state level. In addition, the complexity of health care reform as it was proposed in Missouri as well as by the White House, severely limited the ability to engage a wide audience in the debate. The rise and fall of Missouri's ShowMe Health Reform Initiative provides interesting lessons and cautions for states attempting to push a comprehensive health care reform agenda in too short a time. When legislators serve on a part-time basis and have limited knowledge of the issues under debate, the intricacies of comprehensive legislation provide many opportunities for the dissemination of misinformation that soon ends up controlling the legislative debate. The authors point out that states that have succeeded in comprehensive reform efforts have spent years educating legislators and policymakers and building constituencies.

Benjamin Chu's paper "The Role of Graduate Medical Education Consortia in the Postregulatory Era in New York State," provides an interesting and timely history of how New York State's Health Care Reform Act of 1996 was developed and passed. The demise of national health care reform and a new political and policy environment provided a unique window of opportunity for major change agents in New York State to challenge the usefulness of such bedrock issues as the state's highly regulated hospital rate-setting program and traditional funding of GME in a more competitive, market-oriented health care marketplace. Pitched but constructive battles and backroom trading finally resulted in the Health Care Reform Act of 1996, described by the author as "a grand set of compromises that preserved a good deal of the current system while charting new waters."

Passage of the Health Care Reform Act of 1996 in New York State showed that significant reform around an issue where most of the major politically powerful stakeholders had a preponderant financial stake in maintaining the status quo is difficult but achievable. In the end, however, the inertia against change was overcome not so much by data and good information but by the revolution sweeping the organization and financing of health care across the country. According to the author, although information was necessary for change, two major forces represented the keys to final success: the ascendancy of a newly elected state leadership which ran on a compelling reform agenda, and the realities of the new health care environment. In the final analysis, information helped to frame the debate, but political and financial realities created the environment that forced key stakeholders to take stock of their new positions and come prepared to compromise.

In "Information Trading, Politics, and Funding for the National Institutes of Health in the 104th Congress," David Stevens offers a highly informative glimpse into the political process that drives biomedical research in an era of limited budgets. In the new environment even an icon of the American health care system like NIH will have to demonstrate value-added performance. The politics of biomedical research funding are now sharply focused on a debate between the merits of earmarked research funding versus those of investigator-initiated funding. Budget constraints and the dramatic expansion of knowledge in basic biomedical science will in the future create a heightened struggle between powerful research factions competing for limited dollars. The paper suggests that traditionally favored and protected constituencies on Capitol Hill can no longer assume that past largesse will continue into the future. Many of the stakeholders in the biomedical and clinical research communities are already developing ways to develop information and positions more reflective of the changed political and budget environments.

Pearl O'Rourke's paper, "Gene Mapping and Genetic Testing, Promises and Problems: A Case Study on an Emerging Technology," provides a compelling case study on the panoply of information challenges related to educating decisionmakers and the public on a complex and technical issue. Gene mapping and genetic testing have become front-burner issues since passage of the Kassebaum-Kennedy Health Insurance Reform Bill (S.1028) in 1996. The legislation, which provides for portability of insurance coverage, also prohibits exclusion from coverage on the basis of preexisting conditions. The bill specifically prohibits exclusion from coverage on the basis of genetic testing. Lobbying activities related to the Kassebaum-Kennedy legislation provided ample opportunity for public airing of issues focused on discrimination on the basis of genetic information. According to the author, the debate on genetic information and insurance discrimination has attracted "educators" from the insurance industry, the genetic research community, the biotechnology industry, and consumer groups. None of these groups is monolithic. Each has its own agenda. For example, as genetic information is becoming a household concept the research community wants to make sure that the public is on its side. The biotechnology industry's information campaign is focused on the right of Americans to have access to genetic testing, preventing insurance discrimination on the basis of test findings, and limiting the hand of federal regulation over the industry. The information of most interest to consumers focuses on how genetic information is being used to discriminate against individuals with disabling conditions and health risk factors. The insurance industry finds itself trading information in the interest of uniform regulatory requirements across states and assuring the public that only limited genetic information derived from specific laboratory tests might be subject to special premiums. Therefore, around an emerging, poorly understood, and polarizing issue, Congress may find itself in a virtual Tower of Babel. In areas of policy formulation where information is often used to champion a cause, the challenge is to raise the level of independent and objective data that may contribute to more informed legislative resolutions. In addition, the author suggests that the debate in the 104th Congress around genetic information as it relates to insurance discrimination highlights the importance of identifying the precise questions and problems that need to be addressed. In its absence, the dialogue gets diffused and distracted by other, competing issues.

"The Information Trading Process: The Case of Medicare Payment Equity," by Susan Bartlett Foote, provides a number of valuable perspectives on the information trading process as it unfolds on Capitol Hill. The author identifies three key players: the producers of information, the consumers of information, and the information agents. Often derided as "special interests" or "mere lobbyists," at their best they can help to interpret and translate a complex and highly technical knowledge base and serve as catalysts to convert policy research into policy results. From the perspective of having played all three roles, Susan Foote reflects on information trading as it has unfolded around the current debate around payment inequities in Medicare's average adjusted per capita costs (AAPCC). In the case of AAPCC, the major stakeholders have had a special interest in keeping the issue under wraps, given the significant and for the most part adverse financial consequences of any change. Plans advocating a fairer and more equitable payment formula had to "get the story out," do important coalition building and hone a compelling message in the context of current congressional debate related to Medicare reform and budget reductions. From her key role in developing the Fairness in Medicare Coalition, the author offers three important points for any new group wanting to become an effective player and voice for change: (1) welcome the opportunity to testify at a public hearing—being a witness gives a group new on the scene important visibility among the trade press and key members of Congress; (2) develop principles and guidelines for what the group wants to accomplish, but maintain some flexibility as various legislative proposals are drafted; and (3) develop a cadre of dedicated champions.

Anyone interested in public policy and affecting the policy process will find valuable lessons and pointers in this volume. The art of information and information trading in a political environment, while ever changing, continues to be a fascinating if not always edifying reality of the legislative process.

1
The Market for Information in Health Policy:
Using the "Just-in-Time" Strategy

Wendy B. Young

Information is the raw ingredient supplying the public policy process. Throughout the process of policymaking, information is traded and transformed by participants seeking to influence the process and emerging policy. In the past two decades, the supply of information available to inform public policy has expanded and diversified in response to an increase in competition and partisanship in the policymaking process.

A dramatic new development, fueled by congressional committee restructuring in the 1970s and 1980s, that emulates trends in the manufacturing industries, is occurring in information trading. The increasingly competitive and partisan environment and the subsequent desire for an ever-shortening response time prompts participants in the policymaking process to seek strategies that quickly sort the excess information that they receive and customize the information into a product that they can use immediately to advance their targeted message of the moment. Participants in the public policymaking process are making the same discovery as Japanese manufacturers: just-in-time (JIT) management strategies can shorten production time and enhance market competition. Policymakers are using think tanks, interest groups, and lobbyists to supply ready-to-use information, outsourcing background work traditionally supplied by congressional and executive branch agencies. In turn, the growing distance between policymakers and these executive branch agencies whose programs generate the data used by external information suppliers to create customized information products, is putting these agencies' budgets at risk and reducing the capacity for intramural and extramural evaluation of federal health care programs.

THE JIT MANUFACTURING STRATEGY AT TOYOTA

With the advent of JIT strategies, the process of supplying information to health policymakers is taking on characteristics of the Japanese manufacturing process. U.S. policymakers and Japanese automakers are using JIT strategies to manage excess supply, shorten production time, increase flexibility, spread their risk to suppliers, and reduce cost. Just as the JIT manufacturing strategy has helped Japanese manufacturers expand their market share, policymakers using the JIT strategy are seeking a competitive edge for influencing policy proposals and political agendas. A look at how JIT manufacturing works at Toyota, the most cited example of the widespread use of the JIT strategy in manufacturing, highlights the attractive features of these strategies: reducing excess supply, timeliness, more flexibility, shared risk, and reduced cost (Schonberger, 1982).

A Response to Excess Supply

Japanese manufacturers adopted the JIT strategy when they realized that their suppliers had overproduced the required products and created an excess capacity (Schonberger, 1982). When steelmakers overproduced steel, Japanese manufacturers decided that they no longer needed to stock steel or make their own components to keep their production times from being slowed by gaps in the supply of steel parts. Although eliminating their stock increased manufacturers' dependence on their suppliers, they compensated for this by eliminating the waste that resulted from transporting, storing, and cataloging materials.

Timeliness

The JIT strategy drastically reduces the timeline from product design to customer delivery by outsourcing the components (Bowman and Kogut, 1995). Toyota is as much as 1.5 years faster than any U.S. or German carmaker at bringing a car with a new design to market (Smith, 1995). Simultaneous engineering gives suppliers the same time to change the components as the assembly plant has to change the production process. The car design as well as its parts can be modified throughout development, because suppliers participate in the creation of the idea and the design of the car that results from that idea (Dale, 1994). The new product emerges into the market in time to match changing customer tastes and gives Toyota a market advantage before other carmakers have comparable products.

Flexibility

The JIT strategy increases flexibility by closing the supply market. Each essential component has one exclusive supplier. There is no competitive bidding process. Toyota supplies are customized components, tailor-made for each car design. Suppliers continuously refine their components by roaming the assembly plant and talking with workers about potential improvements in the assembly process or the performance of their components. Either a component is ready to use (arrives at the moment and location in the assembly line process where it is to be installed and works properly) or the assembly worker and supplier change the component or the assembly process.

Shared Risk

Extensive outsourcing to sole contractors puts suppliers at the same risk as manufacturers for product failure, a benefit for manufacturers who grant exclusive contracts. More than 70 percent of Toyota's components are outsourced (Smith, 1995). Suppliers share the responsibility for meeting the production quotas set by the manufacturer. In turn, suppliers are given complete access to the assembly process and workers and a preferred operation site in close proximity to the assembly plant that they supply. These exclusive suppliers also have exclusive contracting rights to supply all sub-components and other less frequently used parts obtained from subsuppliers. The manufacturer shares with these exclusive suppliers its savings from reducing production time, improving quality, and increasing market share (Smith, 1995).

The car assembly plant in Toyota City is the hub of consecutive rings of suppliers located according to Toyota's dependence on them (Smith, 1995). The innermost ring contains the sole engine supplier, whose close proximity makes it possible to deliver a load of engines every 20 minutes at the dock adjacent to the engine assembly station. Located in the next ring are suppliers of essential parts to the major suppliers, such as those making engine parts. The outer ring provides space for marginal subsuppliers who operate on their own timetable to sell to any customer a set of standard components.

Reduced Cost

The cost of production of goods of very high quality is less when the JIT strategy is used (Schonberger, 1982). By relying on suppliers to deliver goods for assembly on a JIT basis, the costs of bidding for, packaging, storing, and wasting defective or excess supplies are eliminated rather than just being passed along the supply chain. Also, a faster product assembly time lowers labor costs. Streamlining customer delivery also lowers labor costs. For example, in the United States WalMart is using JIT strategies to save one third of its costs by moving goods directly from the manufacturer to the store shelf (McInerney and White, 1995).

THE JIT STRATEGY IN THE U.S. CONGRESS

Over the past two decades, the restructuring of congressional committees and increasing ease of travel between home districts and the Capitol have erased any earlier clear distinction between campaigning and policymaking activities. Members of Congress are readily accessible to constituents and can engage in the policy-making agenda of most committees, so they must have information that is current and framed to be consistent with their platform. An information industry has emerged to supply such tailored information on a just-in-time basis. However, this industry is overproducing, so that the supply of information has exceeded the need at any given moment, and created even more reliance on JIT strategies to sort and retrieve only the information needed at the moment.

Growing Demand for Information Creates Excess Supply

The restructuring of Congressional committees in the 1970s and 1980s set off a dramatic transformation of the public policymaking process (Ricci, 1993; Smith, 1988). Prior to 1970 seniority and specialization determined committee appointments, giving policy-making order and consistency. Over several terms on the same committee, members and their staffs became experts in a policy specialty and trained new committee appointees. Adequate information was available from congressional and executive branch resource offices, and this information generally fit the information needs of each committee. Without the ease of jet travel, representatives and senators stayed in Washington during the session, so that their information and support network were their political party, committee member and staffs, and colleagues (Smith, 1988).

The growth of jet travel in the 1970s put constituents in immediate contact with their representatives and senators, and members of Congress spent more time in their districts. Greater constituent contact led to more focus on one's own agenda, and as television coverage of congressional activities grew in the 1970s, individual members could readily promote their own agendas (Smith, 1988).

The restructuring of congressional committees, which dismantled traditional committees and created new subcommittees, opened the committee appointments so that even new members could realistically campaign for committee seats to promote their agendas (Ricci, 1993). Committee appointments and agendas were no longer controlled by party, tenure, specialization, and loyalty (Ricci, 1993; Smith, 1988).

Opening the committee appointments dispersed power and expanded the agenda as the policymaking process engaged more participants and a wider range of perspectives (Ricci, 1993; Smith, 1988). All committee and subcommittee members acquired staff, and the staff expanded the agenda to showcase the member and the member's special issues (Smith, 1988). Members of special interest groups could now promote their goals by supporting a certain member of Congress for key committee appointments. The market for policy information grew from the relatively permanent and exclusive group of staff serving a few senior members of Congress to a large and diverse range of staff serving each member of Congress who expressed interest in a particular policy issue. Individual members constructed their own fleet of consultants to advise them on, for example, media, strategy, polling, and direct mail replacing the political party organization's traditional role (Smith, 1988). Washington, D.C., thus began to see a proliferation of advocacy, lobbying, consulting, and think tank organizations seeking to supply information to those involved in an expanded and more diverse policymaking process (Knoke, 1990; Smith, 1988). For example, conservatives created their own think tanks (e.g., the Heritage Foundation and the Cato Institute) to compete with well-established liberal and moderate operations (Ricci, 1993).

As more outside groups participated in the policymaking process, the staffs of members of Congress and committee staffs became flooded with the explosion of materials supplied by this growing information industry. Congressional offices expanded their staffs to keep up with the growing agenda and information, and their growth expanded the agenda further, stimulating a new supply of information products (Smith, 1988). The information supply grew to become excessive, disorderly, and dissonant; it was no longer orderly and consonant with the needs of members. The nature and work of congressional staff leaves them ill equipped to sort and store the voluminous and conflicting information that they received on any policy subject. With an endless new supply arriving daily, information products became something used at the moment for the current political agenda or discarded.

I became aware of the information explosion as it related to health care policy almost instantly when I began work for Senate Minority Leader Tom Daschle as a 1995–1996 Robert Wood Johnson (RWJ) Health Policy Fellow. The amount of mail and other correspondence related to health care issues was a pile of material at least a foot high that arrived daily and was distributed somewhat randomly by the office interns into the mailboxes of the two health legislative assistants and me. Each piece was passed along to the other two members of the team involved with health-related issues, who could keep material of special relevance or interest and toss the rest. I quickly learned to save material relevant to the stage of an issue at the moment and toss anything else. The amount of mail was too large to catalog for later retrieval. Anything that became relevant at a later date could be retrieved from the source or, more readily, from a group advocating the issue. For example, I filed all the mail that we received on medical savings accounts during the health insurance reform debate. I did not, however, attempt to save all the mail that we received on various provisions of Medicare and Medicaid reform. I relied instead on the Center for Budget and Policy Priorities, some key foundations, Families USA, and a few other groups for up-to-date summaries that supported our office's agenda.

Rising Value of Timeliness

The value of timeliness is increasing as the debate on a specific topic expands and becomes more competitive. Differences between campaigning and policymaking are becoming blurred. The continuous contact with constituents and the all-important and frequent media coverage, especially via C-SPAN, has members of Congress constantly campaigning (Smith, 1988). All stakeholders, public officials, and private interests are in a constant race to create from events the opportunity to advance their political agenda (Kingdon, 1995).

Congressional staff have discovered that outsourcing can shorten the time that they take to produce policy and political materials to advance the message of the moment. Beyond the thorough, objective problem and policy analyses that they obtain from congressional and executive branch offices (Congressional Research Service, General Accounting Office, Physician Payment Review Commission, Prospective Payment Assessment Commission, and legislative staff of the U.S. Department of Health and Human Services [DHHS]), and the budgetary analyses that they receive from the Congressional Budget Office and the Office of Management and Budget, congressional office staff who work on health issues rely on a selected group of think tanks and interest groups for information (Knoke, 1990). These outside information traders supply within a day or two targeted information products that are ready to use for a legislative provision, floor debate on alternative proposals, or talking points for a press conference to propose new legislation.

As an RWJ fellow working on the many versions of Medicaid reform proposals, I developed a short list of interest groups and think tanks to supply me with a quick answer, rebuttal, or response to fit into a memo, talking point, chart, or brief remarks that I needed to draft within a few hours or a day. One strategy crafted to oppose the May 1996 Republican Medicaid reform provisions as part of the welfare reform movement highlighted how the proposed changes in Medicaid would make Medicare benefits inaccessible for many vulnerable dually eligible senior citizens. Although the data were checked with DHHS legislative staff, the Kaiser Family Foundation and Center for Budget and Policy Priorities were called on for the information required to craft the message. Reliance was also placed on the Center for Budget and Policy Priorities for an analysis of the total combined federal and state funding cuts in the Republican Medicaid block grant proposal.

Interdependence: Trading Political Cover for Inside Tips

Capitol Hill is surrounded by a series of consecutive rings of information suppliers whose proximity to the Hill is relative to the interdependence (Knoke, 1990) similar to the rings of suppliers surrounding the Toyota manufacturing plant. Those highly interdependent with congressional offices share the most risks with these offices. Think tanks and interest groups that are among a congressional office's preferred sources for timely and tailored information products gain advance notice of intended tactical and legislative changes. They also stand ready to deliver tailored information products on an on-call basis. Think tanks that produce information that leans toward one ideological side of an issue and is tailored for the needs of a select group of congressional offices are vulnerable to charges of using methodologies to support the think tank's and congressional members' preconceived views of the issue. Think tanks sometimes bolster their own recommendations by criticizing conflicting information dispensed by other think tanks as based on flawed methodology produced by a group whose beliefs are too strong to see the truth. These think tanks also face the risk to their continuing existence that depends on an ideological balance within Congress to stimulate a bipartisan debate in need of further information.

The think tanks and interest groups offer congressional offices political cover by taking credit for controversial tactics in order to protect the image of a member of Congress (Smith, 1988). They can create a safe moderate position for an elected official by strongly advocating or opposing a more radical position and then agreeing publicly to graciously support the representative's or senator's "astute and prudent" compromise. During the 1996 health insurance reform debate, mental health advocacy groups pushed very strongly for prohibiting any distinction of insurance benefits for mental health coverage from other benefits. When the bill moved to conference committee to resolve differences between the House and Senate versions, these groups formed a coalition to publicly support members who advocated the compromise: no differentiation in annual and lifetime caps. These mental health advocacy groups were in constant communication with the Daschle and other Senate offices during conference committee negotiations. As part of the many conversations with these groups' representatives, they were kept up to date on the trade-offs under consideration on all provisions of the health insurance reform bill, not just the mental health provision.

The think tanks and interest groups that work closely with congressional office staff condense information from research reports, government reports, polls, and the news media and tailor it to fit into the congressional office's political message. These customized information packages relieve congressional staff from trying to quickly read and interpret comprehensive information from objective sources and reshape it to fit the message of the moment. These products, which are delivered quickly, speed up the response time for congressional offices and make it possible to issue new messages that day before the key television or print deadline.

Representative John Kasich, an Ohio Republican and chairman of the House Budget Committee, recently told a *Chicago Tribune* reporter that he relied on the Heritage Foundation and a few other right-wing groups to prepare his arguments for defunding the Overseas Private Investment Corporation (Warren, 1996). Located four blocks from the U.S. Capitol, the Heritage Foundation is a think tank that emerged in the 1970s when congressional restructuring broadened the debate to include more conservative policy alternatives (Ricci, 1993). The Heritage Foundation is a prototype for using the JIT strategy to supply information to individuals involved in the policymaking process. The typical Heritage Foundation information product is a "brief," which is a one-page statement promoting a policy proposal or a preferred explanation of a social problem. Heritage Foundation staff produce briefs by taking background information from reports by university researchers, federal agencies, news media, and polls and condensing and casting the information to fit the preferred political message. These briefs are marketed to conservative congressional offices, whose staff can copy or extract the material to fit the proposal or message that the member wants to support. The Heritage Foundation also supplies information products to Republican Party organizations for public issue and election campaigns (Ricci, 1993; Toner, 1996).

Outer-Ring Information Production

Most university and independent research and policy centers with expertise in social and health problems are outside the beltway (the highway around Washington, D.C., delineating what is perceived to be an insular political and social world), making their role in the policy information market resemble that of the universal parts subsuppliers located farther from the hub of the Toyota assembly plant. They neither seek nor desire the interdependencies that inner-ring think tanks have built with congressional offices. Their products are objective, comprehensive analyses that demonstrate the current status and trends of a social problem or that evaluate the effectiveness of public programs. Their information products stimulate awareness within the congressional and executive branches of social problems that may benefit from program and policy changes. Articles in the *Journal of Pediatrics* or the *Journal of Health and Social Behavior,* just to give two examples, are more likely to be used by think tanks and lobbying groups to support their positions than to be read by congressional staff looking for ideas on new legislation. The products of most university researchers provide the raw material that is modified and extracted by think tanks and interest groups in closer proximity to the Congress that feed the daily information market on a JIT basis. The distance between most researchers and Capitol Hill and researchers' focus on objectivity and thoroughness carve out for them a more peripheral contribution to the moment-by-moment policy and political efforts on the Hill.

Federal Deficit Reduction:
Downsizing, Privatizing, and JIT Strategies

Public interest in reducing the deficit and the proclivity to look toward the private market rather than government for solutions have resulted in numerous changes in the information that is produced by the federal government (Donahue, 1989). Along with White House initiatives to downsize government (Gore, 1993), the 104th Republican Congress's downsizing initiatives ranged from privatizing the

House beauty and barber shops and food services to eliminating the Office of Technology Assessment (OTA) and significantly reducing the budget for the Agency for Health Care Policy Research (AHCPR). In addition, the growing privatization of Medicare and Medicaid through managed care capitation contracting reflects the current thinking that private enterprises are more cost-effective than public operations.

Beyond the general interest in reducing federal spending, policymakers' growing reliance on JIT information products places federal agencies like OTA and AHCPR at special risk and eased the closure of OTA. In the heat of the moment, when the pace of policy action is extremely rapid and the stakes are the highest, congressional offices may be more dependent on outside think tanks and interest groups for the quick, tailored information needed to supply the political message of the moment. The essential value of OTA's comprehensive study reports delivered to Congress within a year or two of a committee's request may be overlooked when attention is directed toward deficit reduction and downsizing (Coates, 1996). Congressional offices receive OTA and AHCPR products frequently through their secondary use, since these federal agencies' products are often recycled because their information is used by such well-respected entities as the Institute of Medicine and universities to inform and strengthen their work (Coates, 1996). OTA data, conclusions, and policy recommendations are also frequently cited in targeted message-oriented paragraphs prepared on request by inside-the-beltway think tanks and interest groups for a congressional member's statement or proposal planned for later that day.

On top of the inherent difficulties in producing for congressional members comprehensive research or analysis within the typical 60-day to 6-month window of attention for a specific issue, reports by OTA and AHCPR can yield findings and recommendations that are more favorable to one special interest than another. Regardless of how sound the methodology and how balanced the range of stakeholders are on a study commission, federal agencies that produce partisan recommendations or find one rationale as a better explanation than another are at risk of incurring the displeasure or even the active opposition of politicians and powerful stakeholders who stand to lose if the study's findings are implemented. AHCPR's back pain study that documented the lack of better outcomes from more expensive surgical rather than less expensive medical treatment spurred an intensive lobbying campaign that resulted in congressional proposals for radical funding reduction and even the elimination of this agency by the 104th Congress. The next year, AHCPR moved away from promulgating clinical practice guidelines, and encouraged external think tanks and private-sector research centers to continue this work.

CONSEQUENCES OF JIT STRATEGIES FOR HEALTH POLICY

The current partisan policy environment of continuous campaigning fueled by the JIT supply of customized information products is reducing the public's role from that of a stimulus for Congress to make policy to that of a consumer of policy made by Congress (Ricci, 1993). The public has been relegated to the role of customer and policymaking is acquiring more marketing characteristics. Although JIT sources provide congressional offices with timely and ready-to-use information for their partisan policymaking activities, the feedback loop between Congress and the inside-the-beltway operators emphasizes political receptivity more than policy effectiveness. The focus often leans more toward what sells, not what lasts. The capacity to evaluate policy effectiveness is at risk from the growing disinterest in maintaining the federal infrastructure that monitors federal health policy. Competing interest in balancing the budget and downsizing the government seeks to eliminate, downsize, or privatize the federal agencies and programs that produce and analyze the data needed to evaluate the consequences of changes in federal health programs and the transformation of the health care delivery system (Gaus and Fraser, 1996).

Medicare claims data, for example, will diminish in size and representation as the Health Care Financing Administration (HCFA) approves more managed care contracts for capitation rather than fee-for-service payment. The General Accounting Office (1996) recently emphasized the need for HCFA to collect individual patient encounter and satisfaction data from health maintenance organizations as the Medicare claims database erodes. Although the claims database has many limitations, especially for determining differences in client satisfaction and outcomes, it has been the primary data set for identifying unnecessary regional variations in cost, utilization and treatment patterns (U.S. Congress, Office of Technology Assessment, 1994). The Medicare claims database provided the data for AHCPR's first round of medical effectiveness studies, the Patient Outcome Research Teams.

As HCFA director in the late 1980s, William Roper looked to AHCPR to be part of the expanded federal infrastructure necessary to evaluate health outcomes in the future as services moved out of the hospital setting and health plans shifted from the fee-for-service system to one of managed care (Roper, 1996). Since then, AHCPR has had diminished capacity as Congress has leaned toward expecting the private-sector market to regulate itself. Although the private sector is generating quality and outcomes data, these self-reported data are not uniformly available and lack external validity, comparability, and standardization across demographic differences (Roper, 1996; Physician Payment Review Commission, 1995). Just after the Physician Payment Review Commission called for a strong research infrastructure to support and improve the development and use of practice guidelines (Physician Payment Review Commission, 1995), Congress deleted from the Conference Committee Report on Medicare Reform the Medicare reform provisions of the Balanced Budget Act of 1995 (H.R. 2491) requiring Medicare choice plans to report aggregate encounter data on physician visits, nursing home days, home health days, inpatient days, and rehabilitation services. Congressional sentiment continues toward privatization and self-regulation and away from a major federal role in quality monitoring. Private funding for large-scale, objective, comparable research will be increasingly critical to evaluating the impact of the changes occurring in public- and private-sector health programs and services (Gaus and Fraser, 1996).

CONCLUSION

Beginning with the restructuring of the U.S. Congress in the 1970s, the environment for policymaking has become increasingly diverse and more partisan. With more committee appointments, members have more podiums to advance their own agendas. They use these to advance two goals: campaigning and policymaking. The shorter policymaking work week, due to the ease of jet travel back to the member's district, and expanded television exposure have increased the value of each moment in the week. JIT information supply helps congressional staff to shorten preparation time to increase the number of opportunities for member's public exposure. A preferred small network of think tanks and interest groups loyal to a member of Congress's agenda serves as an extension of the office staff in their daily work.

Congressional and executive branch resource offices provide the extensive, objective, bipartisan background and analyses that congressional committee and personal staff use to develop legislative proposals. JIT sources, however, are becoming the more common supplier of the customized, ready-to-use information that congressional office staff need to prepare the daily partisan and strategy work.

The popularity of JIT sources may be reinforcing the shift toward privatization and downsizing and eroding the federal capacity for conducting thorough evaluations of its policies. The evaluation of federal health policy and concurrent changes in the private health care sector may fall increasingly to the private sector to fund and conduct, with fewer public data being available to support this work.

REFERENCES

Bowman, E.H., and B.M. Kogut. 1995. Redesigning the Firm. New York: Oxford University Press.

Coates, V.T., 1996. Rebuilding the Office of Technology Assessment. The Chronicle of Higher Education, Section B, p. 4, November 1.

Dale, B.G., ed. 1994. Managing Quality, 2nd ed. New York: Prentice-Hall.

Donahue, J.D. 1989. The Privatization Decision: Public Ends, Private Means. New York: Basic Books.

Gaus, C.R., and I. Fraser. 1996. Shifting paradigms and the role of research. Health Affairs 15(2):235–241.

General Accounting Office. 1996. Medicare: Federal Efforts to Enhance Patient Quality of Care. Report to the Chairman, Subcommittee on Health, Committee on Ways and Means, House of Representatives (Pub. No. GAO-HEHS-96-20). Washington, D.C.: General Accounting Office.

Gore, A. 1993. From Red Tape to Results: Creating a Government That Works Better and Costs Less. New York: Times Books, Random House. (Reproduced in entirety from the U.S. Government Printing Office document.)

Kingdon, J.W. 1995. Agendas, Alternatives, and Public Policies, 2nd Ed. New York: Harper Collins.

Knoke, D. 1990. Political Networks: The Structural Perspective. New York: Cambridge University Press.

McInerney, F., and S. White. 1995. The Total Quality Corporation. New York: Truman Talley Books.

Physician Payment Review Commission. 1995. Annual Report to Congress. Washington, D.C.: Physician Payment Review Commission.

Ricci, D.M. 1993. The Transformation of American Politics: The New Washington and the Rise of Think Tanks. New Haven, Conn.: Yale University Press.

Roper, W. L. 1996. "Can the Marketplace Assure Quality of Care?" Pp. 39–47 *in* The Richard and Hinda Rosenthal Lectures, 1994–1995: Looking Back, Looking Forward: "Staying Power" Issues in Health Care Reform. Washington, D.C.: National Academy Press.

Schonberger, R.J. 1982. Japanese Manufacturing Techniques: Nine Hidden Lessons in Simplicity. New York: Free Press.

Smith, H. 1988. The Power Game: How Washington Works. New York: Ballantine.

Smith, H. 1995. Rethinking America. New York: Random House.

Toner, R., 1996. Interest groups take new route to Congressional election arena. New York Times, pp. A1, A10, August 20.

U.S. Congress, Office of Technology Assessment. 1994. Identifying Health Technologies That Work: Searching for Evidence (Pub. No. OTA-H-608). Washington, D.C.: U.S. Government Printing Office.

Warren, J. September 29, 1996. GOP's budget guy is mostly right, sometimes right on. Chicago Tribune, Section 2, p. 2.

2

Funding Graduate Medical Education in the Year of Health Care Reform: A Case Study of a Health Issue on Capitol Hill

Oliver Fein

In the beginning, there was the Clinton Health Security Act (Clinton HSA). Toward the end, there was the Mitchell bill. Then there was nothing. The year was 1994. Graduate medical education (GME) funding was merely a sideshow in the unfolding drama of health care reform. But it was the crucible in which academic medicine forged its relationship to President Clinton's plan for health care reform. This paper traces the evolution of this health policy issue in the U.S. Senate (see Figure 2.1 on how a bill becomes law) as witnessed by one participant-observer. As the paper follows the peregrinations of GME reform through the Senate, it will focus on the sources of information that shaped the final bill and its outcome.

THE CLINTON HEALTH SECURITY ACT

On January 3, 1994, when I started my Robert Wood Johnson Health Policy fellowship in the Office of Senator George Mitchell, Democratic Senate Majority Leader from Maine, I was handed a 1,362-page document labeled S.1775 (the Clinton HSA). The Clinton HSA had been *dropped* (legislative lingo for introducing a bill) in the Senate on November 22, 1993. I was told that the Clinton

HOW A BILL BECOMES LAW

FIGURE 2.1   SOURCE: Adapted by Oliver Fein from Arkansas Trial Lawyer Association. Reproduced with permission.

legislative drafters had written the bill so that the Senate parliamentarian would assign it to the Labor and Human Resources Committee, headed by Democratic Senator Edward Kennedy from Massachusetts, who was felt to be sympathetic to its content. Democratic Senator Daniel Patrick Moynihan from New York objected, however, declaring that his committee, the Senate Finance Committee, had jurisdiction because there were Medicare amendments. The Majority Leader, Senator Mitchell, settled the controversy by assigning the bill to both committees, promising to reconcile whatever differences might result from dual assignment by authoring a Mitchell Bill that would be the final product introduced on the Senate floor. One of my first tasks was to review Title III on Public Health Initiatives, which contained the GME sections of the bill. The Clinton HSA did the following:

- Created an all-payer fund for GME and academic health centers (AHCs) of $40 billion over 5 years by pooling GME funds from the Medicare trust fund with a new 1.5 percent assessment on private health insurance premiums (Tables 2.1 and 2.2).
- Established physician workforce policies (Table 2.3),
    –including a statutory mandate that 55 percent of all residents must complete their training in primary care specialties (family medicine, general internal medicine, general pediatrics and obstetrics-gynecology) and;
    –including a National GME Council to reduce the total number of residency training positions so that the total number "bears a relationship to the number of individuals who graduated from medical schools in the United States."
- Distributed the "direct" GME* dollars on the basis of a "na-

---

*In the Clinton HSA, Medicare "direct" GME funds (DME), which cover trainee salaries and fringe benefits, malpractice insurance and supervisory costs were placed into a GME account, whereas Medicare "indirect" GME funds (IME), also called the indirect medical education adjustment, which cover the higher operating costs of teaching hospitals, were allocated to an AHC account. Both accounts were to be financed by a combination of Medicare dollars and a new 1.5 percent assessment on premiums.

TABLE 2.1   Proposed Sources of GME/AHC All-Payer Funds, 1996–2000 (in billions of dollars)

Proposed Source	Medicare, No Change[a]	Clinton HSA[b]	Senate Labor[c]	Senate Finance[d]	Mitchell Bill[e]
Medicare IME	$29	$10	$15	$25	$26
Medicare DME	$8	$8	$9	$9	$12
1.5% of private premiums	$22	$35	$32	$29	
Total	$37	$40[f]	$59[f]	$66[f]	$67[f]
Medicare savings		$19	$13.9	$3.3	$2.5

[a]HCFA projections for the period 1996–2000, based on Medicare/IME payments at the 7.7 percent level.

[b]Congressional budget office (CBO) projections for the period 1996–2000, based on Medicare/IME payments at the 3.0 percent level.

[c]Congressional budget office (CBO) projections for the period 1996–2000, based on Medicare/IME payments at the 5.2 percent level.

[d]Congressional budget office (CBO) projections for the period 1996–2000, based on Medicare/IME payments at the 7.7 percent level.

[e]Congressional budget office (CBO) projections for the period 1996–2001, based on Medicare/IME payments at the 7.7 percent level.

[f]These totals may differ from those in Table 2.2, since they are based on CBO projections rather than specified in legislation.

tional average per resident (trainee) amount," subsequently estimated to be $55,000 per trainee.

- Made GME payments directly to "the approved physician training program."

All four of these proposals were a major departure from existing policies:

- GME had only been supported by Medicare, not private insurance.

TABLE 2.2 Proposed Uses of GME/AHC, All-Payer Funds, 1996–2000 (in billions of dollars)

Proposed Use	Clinton HSA	Senate Labor	Senate Finance	Mitchell Bill[a]
Academic health centers	$17	$42	$42	$42
Graduate medical education	$23	$23	$25	$25
Graduate nurse education	$1	$1	$1	$1
Medical schools	$0	$2	$2	$2
Dental schools			$0.25	$0.25
Public health schools				$0.15
Total	$41	$68	$70.25	$70.4

[a]For the period 1997–2001.

SOURCE: Amounts specified in reported bills. Amounts are rounded.

- In 1992, only 33 percent of residents were expected to complete their training in the primary care specialties, and the total number of residency positions was 43 percent higher than the number of U.S. medical school graduates; that is, they were filled by international medical graduates. In addition, there was no national GME council to allocate resident positions (Kindig and Libby, 1994).
- Direct GME payments varied from $32,358 to $183,369 per trainee. (Association of American Medical Colleges, 1993).
- GME funds were distributed only to teaching hospitals, not to residency training programs.

The Impact of Expert Panels

Where did President Clinton come up with these new ap-

TABLE 2.3   Workforce Proposals in 1993–1995 National Health Care Reform Bills

Policy	Clinton HSA	Labor Committee	Finance Committee	Mitchell Bill
Mandate percentage of generalists	55%	55%	No	55%
No. of residencies in relation to no. of U.S. medical schoolgraduates	Bear a relationship	Bear a relationship	No	See Figure 2.2
National council establishes allocation system	Yes	Yes	No	Yes
Payment method	National average per resident amount	Phase-in "national average" to level of 50%	Medicare historical payment method	Phase-in "national average" to level of 50%

proaches? Table 2.4 lists the expert panels from government, foundations and professional associations that first proposed these changes. Over the years, an impressive base of information and recommendations had been assembled. For example, the Council on Graduate Medical Education (COGME) was created by the U.S. Congress in 1986 and consisted of 17 members drawn from the private sector and government. With the exception of the provision that payments be made directly to residency programs, its Third Report (Council on Graduate Medical Education, 1992) has all the essential elements of the Clinton legislation. COGME states, "All payers should contribute to GME, including Medicare, Medicaid, private insurers, self-insured employee plans, and HMOs [health maintenance organizations] and other managed/coordinated care systems." By including obstetrics-gynecology (OB-GYN) as a primary care specialty (as advocated by Hillary Rodham Clinton), the Clinton HSA proposed 55 percent primary care output, compared to COGME's 50 percent. Rather than adopting COGME's recommen-

TABLE 2.4   Recommended Approaches to Workforce Reform

Expert Panels	Support for 50% Primary Care	Support for Reduction in Total No. of Residents	Support for All-Payer Pool
Council on Graduate Medical Education	X	X	X
Physician Payment Review Commission		X	X
Prospective Payment Assessment Commission	X		X
Pew Health Professions Commission	X	X	X
Robert Wood Johnson Foundation	X		
Macy Foundation	X	X	X
American Medical Association			X
Association of American Medical Colleges	X		X
American Academy of Family Physicians	X	X	X
American Board of Internal Medicine	X	X	X
American Osteopathic Association	X	X	

dation to limit the total number of entry residency positions "to the number of U.S. allopathic and osteopathic medical school graduates plus 10 percent," the Clinton HSA did not use a fixed percentage.

What was the source of the provisions about direct GME payments, in particular, the proposal to make payments to "the approved physician training program"? Again, a congressionally established commission had suggested the language. The Prospective Payment Assessment Commission (ProPAC), which was established to monitor the Medicare program, had recommended a uniform national average per resident (trainee) payment, adjusted for differences in regional wages. ProPAC had also recommended that direct GME payments be made to the residency training program rather than the teaching hospital to encourage more out-of-hospital ambulatory care training. When I arrived in Senator Mitchell's office, the phrase—payment to "the approved physician training program"—was causing substantial agitation among teaching hospitals. It meant that Medicare direct GME payments would be made to training programs, which could then negotiate with teaching hospitals, community health centers, and other sites as training locations. It put the money in the hands of the program directors rather than the chief executive officers of teaching hospitals.

Several outside observers told me that Senator Mitchell's office had played a role in keeping payment to the teaching program language in the Clinton HSA and in excluding a provision that GME funding go through medical school-based consortia. Since the state of Maine has only one small osteopathic medical school, if medical school-based consortia became the only source of GME funding, then medical schools outside of Maine might control GME funding for teaching hospitals in the state. Even though GME consortia were not included in the Clinton HSA, maintaining the provision for direct payment to programs was good insurance against this kind of proposal.

Therefore, I was not surprised to find Dick Knapp from the Association of American Medical Colleges (AAMC) and the Council of Teaching Hospitals (COTH) in my office in January with alternative language to the payment to the teaching program approach: GME payments should be made to "the entity that incurs the cost," which sounded a lot like the status quo—that is, teaching hospitals. Over the spring of 1994, compromise language was crafted in which GME funding went to "the qualified applicant" rather than a specified training program, teaching hospital, or consortium. This appeared to resolve the problem.

It is a testimonial to the significance of private and quasi-governmental expert panels that so many of their recommendations are incorporated into legislative first drafts. The real test of their power, however, is to measure how many of their recommendations survive into enacted legislation. With the failure of the 1994 health reform effort, this ultimate measure of legislative influence cannot be applied.

The Administration as an Information Source

Information from the Clinton Administration was also critical in shaping the issue within Congress. On January 12, 1994, the Office of the Assistant Secretary for Health (OASH) released a briefing memo entitled Academic Health Center and Workforce Policies. It laid down the rationale for all-payer GME financing in terms that sound quite familiar today: "Private insurers now pay major teaching hospitals 25% to 30% more than community hospitals. In a more competitive environment, health plans will not pay additional amounts the way traditional indemnity insurers do today. In a re-formed payment system, we need to provide funds to preserve physician training and quality of care at academic health centers" (U.S. Department of Health and Human Services, 1994). This became the justification for the enormous subsidy for AHCs provided through GME in health reform legislation.

In addition, the Clinton Administration couched its argument for GME reform in a scheme to reduce Medicare spending on GME. The Administration estimated that without the HSA, Medicare would spend a total of $37 billion on GME and AHCs over 5 years. With HSA, this total amount would rise to $40 billion over 5 years, but the Medicare share would drop to $18 billion, resulting in $19 billion of savings for the Medicare program over 5 years (see Table

2.1). The difference would be made up by assessments on the privately insured—a win–win situation for academic medicine and government alike.

Committee Hearings

This was the lay of the "GME-land" when the Senate Finance Committee worked out its schedule of hearings. In fact, congressional hearings rarely change anyone's mind, least of all the senators themselves. They do, however, create a forum for constituency expression and serve to legitimize the ultimate legislative product, whether or not it embraces the testimony. The Finance Committee held 22 hearings on health care over 5 months, a veritable course in health policy. Looking back, however, the marked up bill was not significantly influenced by the hearings.

Finance Committee staff played the dominant role in determining who to invite to present testimony. Senators on the committee could suggest witnesses, but the ultimate choice was made by Chairman Moynihan and his staff. Selections appeared to be based on at least two criteria: the constituency represented by the witness and the witness's home state. The first Senate Finance Committee hearing on GME was held on March 8, 1994. Each of the four witnesses had been carefully selected. Peter Budetti, a pediatrician and lawyer, was director of the Center for Health Policy Research, which is based in Washington, D.C. He did not come from a committee member's state. He was clearly the staff's witness. Jack Colwill, professor and chair of family medicine at the University of Missouri, appeared on behalf of COGME. Debra Folkerts, a family nurse practitioner, represented the American Nurses Association, the American Association of Nursing Colleges, and the National Nurse Practitioner Coalition. It was no coincidence that she came from Kansas, home of the Senate Minority Leader, Robert Dole. Finally, Clayton Jensen, dean of the University of North Dakota School of Medicine, represented community-based medical schools, which produce graduates, more than 50 percent of whom choose primary care. This witness was a bow in the direction of Democratic

Senator Kent Conrad, the committee member from North Dakota. In sum, this hearing was designed to make the case for workforce reform and primary care.

It is a testimony to the effectiveness of Peter Budetti's presentation (as well as his reputation and experience) that, even though he was an advocate for primary care, he was subsequently hired by the Senate Finance Committee to help with the legislative review of issues relating to GME, malpractice, antitrust, and other physician-associated topics.

About 1 month later, on April 14, the committee scheduled the hearing to make the case against workforce reform and primary care, entitled Academic Health Centers under Health Care Reform. Again, the witnesses reflected a variety of constituencies, with a disproportionate number of witnesses from Chairman Moynihan's state of New York. Spencer Foreman, from New York's Montefiore Hospital and Medical Center and past president of the AAMC represented the AAMC. Paul Marks, a personal friend of Chairman Moynihan and president of Memorial Sloan-Kettering Cancer Center in New York, represented subspecialty and scientific medicine. Raymond Schultz, director of the Medical Center at the University of California, Los Angeles, represented teaching hospitals. Stuart Altman, a Brandeis University economist and chair of ProPAC, was the staff's witness.

There was one anomalous witness at the second hearing. Daniel Onion, director of the Maine-Dartmouth Family Practice Residency Program. Although he had an academic affiliation with Dartmouth, Dr. Onion seemed out of place. As he said, "I feel like an onion in the petunia patch," since he was a family physician among high-powered leaders of academic medical centers. The primary reason that Dr. Onion appeared was that he came from Maine, the state of Majority Leader Mitchell. He went on to steal the show with the hearing room audience, if not with the senators, describing how he and a nurse provided cardiopulmonary resuscitation to a ski accident victim while a urologist and orthopedist stood around unable to turn their specialist skills to the general emergency need of the moment. Dr. Onion spoke for establishing a target of 50 percent primary care, in the context of reducing the number of residency positions to 110 percent of the number of U.S. medical school graduates. He also advocated direct payment of GME monies to residency programs.

It was only after the hearing concluded that it was realized how deeply held Chairman Moynihan's views on workforce reform were. When Dr. Onion was reviewing the transcript of his testimony he came across a Moynihan remark that none of us had heard on the day of the hearing: "I do note that under the guise of simplicity he [Dr. Onion] argues that his plain, simple *half herbal* teachings cost half again as much as [training] at Sloan-Kettering." We all knew that Chairman Moynihan had to defend his New York constituency, which trained 15 percent of the nation's residents, even though it has only 7 percent of the nation's population. This bias in attitude toward primary care was widely shared by those closely allied with the nation's top academic medical centers.

THE MARK-UP

The Finance Committee markup of HSA took place in the last week of June 1994 and extended into the Saturday of the July 4th weekend. The markup was conducted in the context of the Labor and Human Resources Committee's release of its final bill on June 9, 1994. Senator Kennedy was viewed as a friend of academic medicine and had reported out a bill that was extremely favorable to academic health centers and that specifically created a new funding pool for medical schools.

The Labor and Human Resources Committee bill provided more funds for GME and AHCs than Clinton's HSA—a total of $68 billion over 5 years, compared with Clinton's $41 billion (see Table 2.2). This included Kennedy's creation of a medical school funding pool that was worth $2 billion over 5 years. The origin of this medical school fund dates back to an October 1993 Saturday morning meeting at the White House of 13 deans from the most prestigious, research-intensive medical schools in the United States. This group, which dubbed itself "the Saturday Morning Working Group," was organized by Michael Johns, dean at Johns Hopkins School of

Medicine, and Herbert Pardes, dean at Columbia University's College of Physicians and Surgeons. They had formed the group because they felt excluded from the Health Reform Task Force and underrepresented by their traditional lobbyist, the AAMC, and so they hired their own lobbyist (Capitol Associates, Inc.). It was clear that the proposal for a $2 billion medical school fund was a product of their efforts.

Senator Kennedy seemed to recognize that if these huge sums of money were to go into physician training then they needed to be accompanied by a workforce policy that emphasized primary care. So the Kennedy bill included the 55 percent goal for primary care and a national council to reduce the number of residency training slots without a specified target. The result of markup in Senator Moynihan's Finance Committee was essentially identical to that in Senator Kennedy's Labor and Human Resources Committee with respect to GME funding levels, but there were no workforce goals for primary care or for reducing the number of residents.

The vote on GME financing in the Finance Committee was tense. Republican Senator Malcolm Wallop from Wyoming, on the basis of the popular Republican platform of opposition to any new taxes, introduced an amendment to eliminate the premium surcharge that was the source for all new funding for GME, AHCs and medical schools. The committee had 20 members—11 Democrats and 9 Republicans. If the Republicans stuck together, it would take only two Democrats to swing the vote in favor of the amendment, and all new funding for GME and AHCs would be dead. The voting always started with the Democratic majority and the ranking member, Democratic Senator Max Baucus from Montana. Like Senator Wallop, he had no medical school in his state, and with no workforce provisions in the bill, Senator Baucus voted in favor of the amendment. Democratic Senator Jay Rockefeller from West Virginia was the wild card. He had always said, "No money for GME/AHCs without workforce reform." However, he voted against the Wallop amendment. Ultimately, only one Democrat voted for the Wallop amendment and three Republicans opposed it. Financing for GME and AHCs was saved, but without workforce provisions.

THE MITCHELL BILL

On Saturday, July 2nd, hours after the Finance Committee had completed its markup, Senator Mitchell gathered his health care-related staff: John Hilley, chief of staff; Bobbie Rosen, his tax man; Lisa Nolan, his budget specialist; Christine Williams, his health care-related legislative assistant; Parashar Patel, a detailee from the U.S. Department of Health and Human Services; and myself. Mitchell said, "When I referred this bill to two committees, I promised my colleagues I would put together my own bill. You have three weeks" (G. Mitchell, pers. com., July 1994). He instructed us to work with staff from both committees and outlined the broad principles he thought we ought to follow.

As we learned later, there was one problem with these orders. The chief of staff of the Finance Committee forbade his staff from meeting with us when members of the Labor and Human Resources Committee staff were present. This contributed to some of the tensions that subsequently developed around GME.

In many respects, the Labor and Human Resources and the Finance Committees had reported out similar GME financing bills. As can be seen on Table 2.1, the dollar amounts for AHCs and GME were the same in both bills. However, the amount of savings for Medicare was substantially larger in the Labor and Human Resources Committee bill compared with that in the Finance Committee bill, since the Labor and Human Resources Committee reduced the Medicare indirect GME adjustment factor from 7.7 to 5.2 percent, whereas the Finance Committee maintained it at the 7.7 percent level that existed then. ProPAC had advocated reducing the indirect GME adjustment factor to 5.2 percent and the Clinton HSA had reduced it to 3.0 percent. Those preparing the Mitchell bill decided not to buck Moynihan on GME financing and accepted the Finance Committee's funding levels.

However, the big difference between the bills was in workforce provisions. The Senate Finance Committee had no workforce provisions, whereas the Labor and Human Resources Committee bill followed the Clinton HSA in recommending 55 percent of residents in primary care and a national commission to establish a system of allocating residency positions (see Table 2.3). The Labor and Human Resources Committee bill also copied the Clinton HSA with a provision that the number of first-year residencies "bear a relationship to the number of U.S. medical school graduates," but did not specify a percentage, like COGME's 110 percent. The Labor and Human Resources Committee departed from the Clinton HSA, which suggested that direct GME be allocated on a "national average per residency (trainee) amount," by recommending a phase-in of the national average to 50 percent of the historical rate and 50 percent of the national average over 4 years. This was a concession to states like New York that historically had direct GME rates that were much higher than the national average.

Moynihan's opposition to workforce provisions was based at a minimum on his need to be responsive to the teaching hospitals and academic medical centers in New York. Every other committee that had reported out a health care reform bill had workforce provisions. How could such a large government subsidy of GME and teaching hospitals be legislated without accountability for the outcome, particularly since many analysts ascribed a substantial part of medical inflation to the overproduction of doctors?

The staff preparing the Mitchell bill, tried to craft a bill that still had workforce integrity, but that would phase in workforce goals more gradually and loosen the legislative constraints on any national commission in the fourth and fifth years, so that there could be flexibility to respond to the unintended consequences that might result from adherence to rigid percentages (see Figure 2.2). Mitchell's staff worked closely with Labor Committee staff and received substantial help from Senator Rockefeller's staff. Mitchell's staff tried to work out compromises with the Finance Committee staff, but it was difficult without being able to get everyone in the same room. Frankly, Mitchell's staff felt that the GME and AHC funding components of the legislation were in jeopardy without the workforce provisions and thought that Senator Moynihan would ultimately see it that way also.

The Clinton Administration's control of data was also significant. As Mitchell's staff rewrote the GME financing sections of the

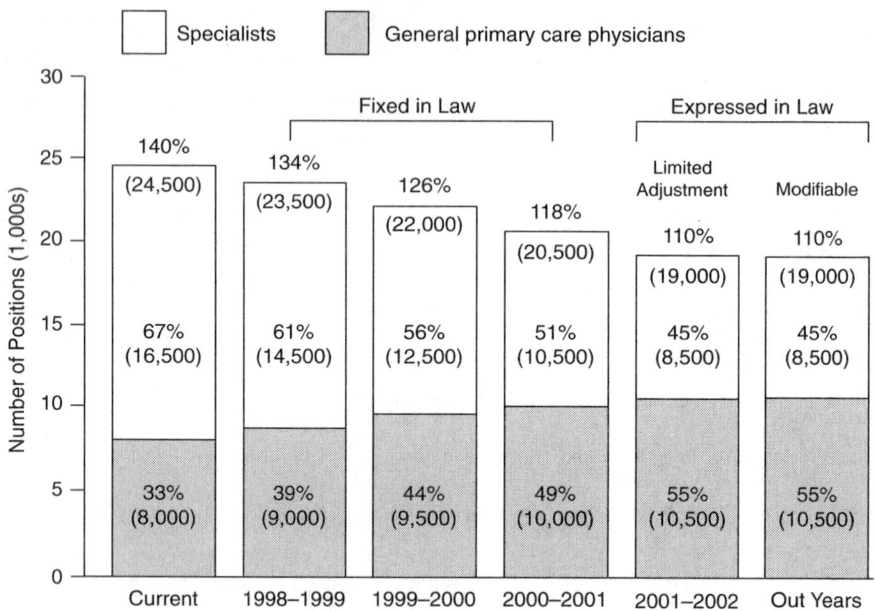

FIGURE 2.2 A flexible proposal to reduce first-year residency training positions. SOURCE: The Mitchell bill.

Mitchell bill, they were interested in the impact of workforce reform provisions, particularly on rural states and New York State. With this information Mitchell's staff might have been better able to speak to Senator Moynihan's fears of an adverse impact on New York. It turned out, however, that these data were viewed as political dynamite by the Clinton Administration, because they showed the wide disparity under existing Medicare formulas in the distribution of GME funds between states (e.g., for every GME dollar spent in North Dakota, $217 was spent in New York). What was worse from the Administration's perspective was that the Mitchell bill increased this disparity (e.g., for every GME dollar spent in North Dakota, $368 would be spent in New York). Thus, the Administration held back on releasing the data until mid-August, when it was too late to influence most senators' positions.

The Senate Floor

The Mitchell bill was introduced in the Senate on August 8th. Senators Moynihan and Kennedy were assigned as floor managers for the bill. When Senator Moynihan vigorously protested the GME and AHC sections of the bill, Senator Mitchell decided to drop the provision on reducing the number of trainees to a percentage of U.S. graduates from the second version of the Mitchell bill.

This did not mollify Senator Moynihan, however, who rose on the Senate floor on Saturday, August 13th, and railed against the remaining workforce provisions, saying: "This invites the wrath of the gods . . . this is a sin against the Holy Ghost." He also added, "There is a staff member somewhere who wants this. And no matter what we do, we keep getting it" (U.S. Congress, 1994). I was floored. Yes, there were many staff members who favored regulation of the physician workforce. There was also the weight of 20 years worth of information molders: private and government expert panels, the record of the other committees in the U.S. House of Representatives that had reported out health reform legislation, and the opinions of multiple senators and representatives, all of whom favored workforce provisions, not to mention the political calculation that if academic medicine wanted $70 billion worth of support (almost twice what it presently received from Medicare) then it would have to accept some accountability for the workforce product.

Senator Moynihan was unyielding. He drew up an amendment that stripped the Mitchell bill of all workforce provisions. As the debate proceeded on the Senate floor, amendments to the Mitchell bill began to be entertained. Amendments alternated between Republican proposals and Democratic proposals. At first, each side offered amendments in which the outcome was clear. This avoided votes that were meaningful in terms of estimating the ultimate support for the bill. Everyone recognized that the Moynihan amendment was different. It was not clear whether the Democrats would stick together in opposing the Moynihan amendment and how many Republicans would support it. If workforce provisions were stripped from the Mitchell bill, would there be majority support for GME and AHC funding? For the Democrats, the Moynihan amendment was a meaningful, defining amendment. Within the Democratic leadership there was substantial debate about when to introduce it. Just at the point that it appeared that a decision had been made to put forward the Moynihan amendment as the next Democratic amendment, the House voted and passed the Crime Bill. Senator Mitchell decided to suspend debate on health care and move the Crime Bill to the Senate floor. Although there was considerable negotiation with the Mainstream Coalition[*] over the ensuing weeks, the Mitchell bill never made it back to the Senate floor. On September 27, 1994, Senator Mitchell announced to the press that health reform was dead.

CONCLUSION

Senator Mitchell often pointed out to his staff that if health reform did not pass in 1994, one consequence would be that everyone would know how to make cuts in Medicare and Medicaid in the future. He predicted that the next Congress would just cut Medicare and Medicaid without expanding coverage for the uninsured. So it was not surprising that Medicare GME funding was on the congressional cutting table all through the 104th Congress. No doubt it will be one of the first items on the agenda for cutbacks in the 105th Congress.

Can anything be learned from the saga of health care reform in 1994? Certainly, the information provided by expert panels and commissions is a significant force in shaping health care legislation. In addition, the role of the Administration's control of the flow of information is important. However, these forces may frame the issue, but they pale in significance compared to the role of interest

---

[*]A group of moderate Republican and conservative Democratic senators that coalesced during the 1994 health care reform effort led by Republican Senators John Chafee of Rhode Island and David Durenberger of Minnesota, and Democratic Senators John Breaux of Louisiana and Ken Conrad of North Dakota. The Mainstream Coalition attempted to chart a programmatic course between the liberal Democrats and the conservative Republicans.

groups. It is striking how much interest groups shape the final product. The deans' Saturday Morning Working Group was able to take the opportunity of national health care reform and insert entirely new support for medical schools. The New York academic health centers were able to exert enormous influence to maintain the status quo, even if it jeopardized enhanced funding for the total enterprise. When these forces combine with the ideological preferences of a powerful member of Congress, then politics overwhelms policy.

In a recently published book, Theda Skocpol (1996), professor of government and sociology at Harvard University, dismisses most conventional explanations for the Clinton failure in health care reform. She feels that President Clinton should have gone for a less regulated system requiring higher taxes. "I conclude," she writes "that President Clinton should have been less worried about pleasing the deficit and budget hawks. He should have done what his conservative critics falsely charged him with doing—acted more like a Democrat in the New Deal tradition, by combining new Federal regulations with generous subsidies to those affected" (Skocpol, 1996, p. 182). Ironically, when it comes to GME funding, the Mitchell bill would have done precisely that. It increased taxes (through an assessment on private health insurance premiums), provided generous subsidies to academic medicine, and established flexible new federal regulations in workforce policy. Academic medicine will not fare as well for the foreseeable future.

POSTSCRIPT

Was any of the "information" generated for the 1994 health reform effort carried over into the 104th Congress? With the Republicans in control, the 104th Congress was looking for ways to slash the domestic budget. The Clinton health reform effort had shown where $19 billion of Medicare savings could be found over 5 years—in GME. GME seemed like a perfect target. Congress could cut GME without perceptibly reducing benefits to individual Medicare enrollees.

The long shadow of Senator Moynihan still hung over the Senate Finance Committee, and the addition of Republican Senator

Alfonse D'Amato from New York only enhanced its effect. The Senate Finance Committee ultimately passed only minor changes. GME funding cuts were limited to $9.9 billion over 7 years and were taken only from indirect GME payments (by reducing the indirect medical education adjustment factor from 7.7 to 4.5 percent), not from direct GME payments, which remained untouched. These cutbacks were ameliorated by a carve-out of GME payments to managed care companies who enrolled Medicare patients into health maintenance organizations, but refused to contribute to the expense of training residents. Workforce policy encouraging primary care or discouraging international medical graduates was not included.

In the House, the Ways and Means Committee was much more radical than the Senate. It cut Medicare's GME support substantially, replacing some of it with funding from general revenues. This maneuver was accomplished by borrowing another Clinton health reform concept, the creation of a GME and an AHC Trust Fund. The GME and AHC Trust Fund received contributions from Medicare and from federal government general revenues instead of Clinton's 1.5 percent assessment on private health insurance. By eliminating payments for trainees beyond first board eligibility, the Ways and Means Committee implicitly adopted a workforce policy that discouraged subspecialty training. By phasing out all funding for non-U.S. citizens, they were essentially limiting federal GME funding to American medical graduates, a much more radical policy than Clinton's.

Of course, all of these proposals were stopped by President Clinton's veto of the Balanced Budget Act of 1995. It is likely, however, that the 105th Congress will revisit these issues earlier rather than later in 1997. Therefore, it is instructive to summarize what the joint Senate and House conference committee adopted and what it rejected. The GME provisions adopted included

• AHC and GME Trust Fund—not an all-payer trust fund, but one that reduces Medicare's contribution by partially replacing it with general revenue funding;
  • cap on the number of residents at the August 1, 1995, level;

and

• reduction of GME payments to 25 percent for trainees after first board eligibility. This primarily effects subspecialty fellowships.

The conference committee rejected

• limit on non-U.S. citizen international medical graduates;
• carve-out of GME funds from Medicare payments to Medicare health maintenance organizations; and
• formation of an Advisory Panel on Reform in Financing of Teaching Hospitals and GME.

Anticipating 1997's congressional debate, the AAMC testified before the House Ways and Means Subcommittee on Health on June 11, 1996. AAMC supported creation of a GME Trust Fund and called for a "shared responsibility approach," another way of saying all-payer financing; limitation of Medicare GME to U.S. medical graduates; and expansion beyond hospitals of the entities that may receive GME payments, such as medical schools, multispecialty group practices, GME consortia, or other entities that incur the costs of training (but not training programs directly), to remove the barriers to training physicians in non-hospital-based ambulatory settings. These will be the GME issues that face the 105th Congress. They all surfaced in the 1994 health care reform effort, and Congress is all the more sophisticated because of it.

REFERENCES

Association of American Medical Colleges. 1993. GME Census. SAIMS Database. Washington, D.C.: Association of American Medical Colleges.

Council on Graduate Medical Education. 1992. Improving Access to Health Care through Physician Workforce Reform: Directions for the 21st Century. Washington, D.C.: U.S. Department of Health and Human Services, Health Resources and Services Administration.

Kindig, D.A., and D. Libby. 1994. How will graduate medical education reform affect specialities and geographic areas? Journal of the American Medical Association 272:37–42.

Skocpol, T. 1996. Boomerang: Clinton's Health Security Effort and the Turn Against Government in U.S. Politics. New York: W.W. Norton.

U.S. Congress. 1994. Congressional Record 140(113):S11667. Washington, D.C.: U.S. Government Printing Office.

U.S. Department of Health and Human Services. 1994. Academic Health Centers and Workforce Policies. Office of the Assistant Secretary for Health, Washington, D.C. January 12. Memorandum.

3
The Use of Information and Misinformation in a State Health Reform Initiative

Robert G. Frank and Coleen Kivlahan

Over the last 60 years, comprehensive reform of the U.S. health care system has been discussed every 10 to 15 years (Frank and VandenBos, 1994). In 1993 and 1994, health reform was discussed in the U.S. Congress and most statehouses. The course of these reform discussions differed, but the discussions were universally accompanied by intense debate in which advocates and proponents predicted radically different impacts of proposed legislation. In some states, such as Washington and Minnesota, major reforms were implemented (Crittenden, 1993; Leichter, 1993). Like the congressional debate, most states struggled with complex health reform issues, only to fail to enact any legislation. Despite the failures, health reform discussions have continued in most states. This paper explores significant factors involved in the failure of Missouri's health reform debate in 1993 and 1994, focusing on the use of information and misinformation in policy decisionmaking and legislative action.

STATE LEGISLATION

In most states, including Missouri, the legislative process and the systems supporting the development of legislation differ from those in the U.S. Congress. State legislative sessions tend to be very short compared with those of the U.S. Congress. For an issue to gain salience in the frenetic and brief state legislative session, it must address a clearly perceived problem, contain a clear solution, and be politically viable (Kingdon, 1984). For an issue to emerge as a piece of legislation that is fully debated, it must be clear, and timing is critical. Despite reports by state legislators and their staff members indicating a significant need for advanced analysis of technical information, most state legislatures have limited access to members of the academic community or think tanks (Guston et al., 1996). Because access to experts is often limited, members of the legislature can gain credence as an "expert" with even limited knowledge about a topic. In Missouri, for example, insurance agents are often seen as more knowledgeable about issues relating to health insurance and coverage for the uninsured than state officials and other traditional experts.

WHY MISSOURI?

Missouri is an excellent laboratory that can be used to obtain an understanding of the development and implications of state health reform initiatives. Located in the center of the nation, Missouri has 5.4 million residents, two large cities (St. Louis and Kansas City), several midsize metropolitan areas, and large rural regions. St. Louis is home to 33 of the nation's largest companies, including Anheuser-Busch, Monsanto, Ralston Purina, and McDonnell Douglas, a fact that heavily influences the regional economy. In addition, the presence of these national and international firms, with strong interests in the role of employers as purchasers of health care services, has a strong influence on the state's approach to health system reform.

The health status indicators of Missouri's citizens, are virtually identical to those for the nation as a whole. Fourteen percent of Missouri's citizens are uninsured, and 63 of the 114 counties are areas federally designated to be experiencing shortages of health professionals. Health care is a $15 billion industry in Missouri. As in other states, Missouri's health care costs have increased over the last two decades. In 1994, both Houses of Missouri's General Assembly were controlled by Democrats, and Mel Carnahan, a Democrat, had just been elected governor. Governor Carnahan's election reversed a 12-year trend during which Republicans held the governor's office. Governor Carnahan had a long history of government service. He had previously served as lieutenant governor, as Missouri state treasurer, and in the General Assembly.

Like many states, Missouri remained mostly untouched by changes in the health services market until 1991. Changes in hospital and purchasing sectors in the St. Louis market heralded transformation for all of Missouri. From 1989 to 1993 the average length of stay dropped from 7.5 to 6.5 days. During the same period, the operating margins and profits of St. Louis hospitals dropped steadily (Katz, 1996). However, from 1991 to the present, urban and rural health care markets have evolved rapidly. In the metropolitan areas, hospitals began the practice of merging with other hospitals. In both St. Louis and Kansas City, three major hospital networks were developing. The merger of Barnes, Jewish, and Christian hospitals in 1993 in St. Louis to form the BJC Health System signaled the rapid onset of significant change in the relationship of hospitals with doctors, rural and community hospitals, and health maintenance organizations (HMOs). Hospital mergers during this period led to the appearance of first generation organized delivery systems: horizontally and vertically integrated health care providers preparing for a capitated financing system. Other evolutionary features included the formation of large metropolitan health coalitions of businesses committed to driving down health care prices by more prudent purchasing of health care for their employees. For example, the St. Louis Business Health Coalition was established in 1982 by the large companies that were members of St. Louis's Civic Progress.

The St. Louis Business Health Coalition was one of the first civic coalitions in the United States to address spiraling health care costs (Katz, 1996). As early as 1987, the St. Louis Business Health Coalition had assembled a report on local hospital performance using data from Medicare cost reports (Katz, 1996). The St. Louis Business Health Coalition developed into a powerful political tool backed by St. Louis's Civic Progress that included the most powerful corporations in St. Louis, indeed in the United States. Because of the corporate powerhouses in St. Louis, the St. Louis Business Health Coalition had access to most elected officials and business leaders.

Other important developments included the growth of the Missouri Consolidated Health Care Plan that promoted movement of public employees into managed care plans, with public employee enrollment in managed care plans growing from less than 10 percent to 75 percent in just a few years. Public employees are located throughout the state, forcing managed care into rural communities at a fast pace. Missouri Medicaid, a $2.5 billion program, recently initiated a capitated managed care system in counties stretching from St. Louis to Kansas City. During the health care reform debates, the Missouri Medicaid program submitted a waiver application under Section 1115 of the Medicaid law to the Health Care Financing Administration to promote policies that would result in a reduction of Missouri's uninsured population.

Before 1990, few legislative initiatives changed Missouri's health care systems (Katz, 1996). In the early 1990s, growth in Medicaid costs became significant. An arrangement with the state's hospitals dramatically increased the disproportionate share funds available to hospitals serving a large number of people who were poor and uninsured. From 1990 to 1993, a series of incremental health reform initiatives were passed. In 1991, a high-risk insurance pool was formed to care for those individuals with devastating pre-existing conditions. In 1992, legislation yielding minor changes in small group insurance practices was implemented. During that legislative session, a small group of vocal advocates paired with a very effective legislator to draw much attention to single-payer models. In 1993, a voluntary medical savings account provision was created. Also in 1993, the Speaker of the Missouri House of Representatives led the effort for the passage of House Bill (H.B.) 564, a broadly constructed piece of health legislation that increased Medicaid eligibility for pregnant women and children to 185 percent of the poverty level, allowed nurse practitioners to work under a collaborative practice agreement with physicians, and provided for enhanced school-based health services statewide. H.B. 564 also included a provision establishing a commission to examine financing of health care through a single payer, market-driven, or other market reform model. The compromise creating this commission reflected the success of single-payer advocates in focusing attention upon needed reform of the health care system. Despite these evolutionary events, in 1994, nearly 600,000 Missouri citizens remained uninsured, an ever-growing Medicaid program accounted for 25 percent of the state's budget, and health care costs continued to grow.

THE SHOWME HEALTH REFORM INITIATIVE

Governor Carnahan was inaugurated in January 1993. The legislative session began shortly after he was inaugurated. Governor Carnahan led successful education reform and joined the Speaker in the effort to pass H.B. 564. During this period, increasing national attention was directed to health reform in response to President Clinton's Health Reform Task Force.

As federal health care reform proposals put forth by the Clinton Administration gained momentum, it became apparent that the state of Missouri was unprepared to evaluate the implications of federal reform proposals. Not only did the state lack a coherent mechanism to evaluate proposed reforms but Missouri also lacked definitive data on the health status of its citizens. In an effort to evaluate the status of health care delivery in Missouri and to design programs that were specific to Missouri's needs, the ShowMe Health Reform Initiative was created. The ShowMe Health Reform Initiative was designed to assess Missouri's health care needs and to design legislation that would allow for the implementation of reforms that complemented Missouri's needs while creating an interface for anticipated federal solutions to health care problems.

To systematically address the problems of Missouri's health care system, a task force of 48 people was created in the summer of 1993. The task force was divided into three work groups. The three work groups addressed issues in health care delivery systems, finance and cost controls, and quality and information systems. During the summer and fall of 1993, the work groups met and reviewed the state of the art in each field. In the fall of 1993, the work groups submitted recommendations for major legislative reform, as well as incremental reform within each area.

The composition of the work groups was carefully planned to reflect the spectrum of political and policy interests usually involved in health care reform issues. The individuals chosen to participate in the various work groups of the ShowMe Health Reform Task Force represented key stakeholders in Missouri's health care industry, health professions, and health care consumer advocates. The composition of the group offered a true cross section of the health care sector. Included on the Task Force were many individuals who had championed opposing views during previous legislative sessions. These individuals were then assigned to work groups without regard to their areas of interest. It was hoped that these collaborative interactions would create a working relationship that facilitated the reform debate.

A series of commissioned papers was developed for each work group to provide the members with current technical information. The acceptance of this role and the development of plans by individuals representing groups that otherwise might have been antagonistic to health care reform were deemed as evidence of substantial progress in an effort to create effective coalitions that would later support the actual legislation. Within the constraints of the short period allowed for this task, there was ample evidence that new relationships developed and a spirit of collaboration ensued. Each work group was able to produce a complex series of recommendations at the appointed time. The recommendations spanned the entire continuum of political ideology, and no effort was made to form a consensus on one solution. Instead, the eventual bill was a compilation of proposals put forth by the work groups. Despite the lack of effort to orchestrate recommendations, the groups produced a number of similar recommendations focusing on critical issues, such as health care workforce, costs, and the quality of health care services.

The recommendations of the work groups were based on materials that were specifically requested for the ShowMe Health Reform Initiative, the existing literature, and most importantly, the knowledge of the members of the working groups. In general, the members of the work groups were extremely knowledgeable and generously contributed their understanding of health care systems issues to the work group.

The Insurance Commission created by H.B. 564 began work several months after the ShowMe Health Reform Initiative had begun. The Insurance Commission included some members of the ShowMe Health Reform Initiative. The Insurance Commission reviewed the documents prepared by the ShowMe Health Reform Initiative. There was frequent conversation between staff and members of the two groups. The Insurance Commission concluded its legislatively chartered agenda in about 8 weeks. Both commissions presented their recommendations to the governor, and a package of systemic reforms was developed.

During the summer of 1993, Governor Carnahan had two health reform commissions operating. One was led by the director of the Department of Health and one was led by the director of the Department of Insurance. These two health reform efforts occurred amid daily news reports on impending federal health reform. The speaker of Missouri's House of Representatives supported additional health reform legislation. Governor Carnahan met routinely with staff of the two health reform initiatives and the directors of the Departments of Health and Insurance. These meetings provided opportunities to review fundamental health reform issues and to discuss legislative priorities.

H.B. 1622

In January 1994, the speaker of the Missouri House of Representatives introduced H.B. 1622. The bill was designed to restructure Missouri's health care delivery and financing system to provide greater access to services and to improve the quality of health care available in Missouri. A comprehensive bill, H.B. 1622, combined a variety of legislative initiatives designed to control costs, provide mechanisms of controlling the growth of health care systems, create standardized indicators of outcomes, enhance consumer information, and enhance accountability for health outcomes measures. H.B. 1622 initiated a gradual transition to community rating by the year 1999. The legislation created three standard benefits plans, with the minimum benefit plan defined as the services available in federally qualified HMOs. Insurers were prohibited from excluding individuals on the basis of preexisting conditions and were not allowed to act as third-party administrators. In addition, the bill created integrated service networks (ISNs), risk-bearing entities licensed as insurance companies that compete on the basis of price and quality. ISNs could be formed by hospitals, physicians, insurers, HMOs, or other entities qualified under state insurance laws. ISNs could not discriminate against any class of medical professionals and were required to use 3 percent of their gross revenues to improve access to health care and public health services.

H.B. 1622 also implemented a number of administrative reforms: creating a Missouri Healthcare Insurance Board responsible for licensing ISNs, establishing the standards for benefits packages, enforcing market rules, determining how to measure quality, and approving technology plans for ISNs. The bill also established the Health Guarantee Corporation, a private corporation established to allow providers and insurers to coordinate their efforts to develop plans to improve community health status, accomplish public health objectives, and develop risk adjustment mechanisms for the ISN premiums and ways to address universal coverage.

INFORMATION AND EDUCATION

Multiple steps were taken to educate Missourians about H.B. 1622 and to ensure that Missourians were involved in the debate. A "health care university" was held for state House and Senate members reviewing complex problems in the health care system and models for health care reform. These symposia were well attended and offered legislators a common understanding of the state's health care system. In addition, the health care university helped develop 10 to 15 leaders on health care issues in the House and Senate. Governor Carnahan held public meetings around the state to describe the health reform bill and to receive public input regarding its contents. Regular press releases and strong interest among the media led to numerous articles and editorials in newspapers throughout the state. Frequent radio and television appearances were made by advocates for H.B. 1622. The two health care commissions, the ShowMe Health Reform Initiative and the Insurance Commission, involved approximately 75 people who worked throughout the summer and fall of 1993 creating principles and specific recommendations. The two commissions' meetings and hearings were attended by hundreds of additional citizens and advocates. The legislature began holding hearings prior to the formal legislative session. Targeted fact sheets regarding the comprehensive legislation were prepared and distributed to all affected individuals, including physicians, hospitals, nurses, other health care providers, employers, and citizens.

The ShowMe Health Reform Initiative commissioned a study by Lewin-VHI (Lewin-VHI, Inc., 1993) that assessed both the number of uninsured citizens in Missouri and potential financing methods to improve access for this group. The results of the study were distributed to the press and to the legislature. The directors of the Departments of Health and Insurance testified for many hours during the legislative session. A bipartisan committee, composed of members of the House and Senate, was formed to further evaluate health reform proposals. The speaker of the House was a strong proponent of universal access and effective health reform. The president pro tem of the Senate was also supportive.

MOVEMENT OF HEALTH CARE REFORM BILLS THROUGH THE GENERAL ASSEMBLY

Prior to the 1994 session, the General Assembly had rarely debated comprehensive health care reform legislation. In 1993, the General Assembly briefly considered several single-payer bills. These were debated rapidly and defeated. In 1993, the General Assembly debated a series of incremental reform bills, passing H.B. 564, which contained a number of independent provisions.

The Missouri legislature, like most state legislatures, is composed of part-time legislators who serve only part of the year. In Missouri, for example, the General Assembly convenes in early January and adjourns in mid-May. As part-time legislators, members of the General Assembly frequently combine their roles as legislators with many other activities. Because the legislators are part-time, they rarely have the ability to develop expertise in an area unless it is related to their occupation. Several key members of the Missouri legislature in the 1994 session were insurance agents. A few other legislators were knowledgeable about health care reform issues, but most had little experience in the area. Thus, within the membership of the General Assembly, there was limited experience with health policy legislation.

State legislatures also typically operate with few staff. Consequently, lobbyists often serve two critical roles: as advocates and as information suppliers. Effective lobbyists, whether advocating or providing information, are viewed by legislators with only a slightly jaundiced eye.

Educating State Legislators

At the beginning of the legislative session, the bill managers were faced with the need to educate 197 members of the legislature, to address the issues needed for passage of the bill, and to manage any misinformation created by opponents of the bill. The General Assembly's limited experience with comprehensive health care reform bills was an important issue. Because of this limited experience, public support was deemed critical in persuading the members of the General Assembly to support the legislation.

Public Opinion

To assess public support, eight focus groups were conducted in critical markets throughout Missouri. In the fall of 1993, focus groups revealed that there was consensus among Missourians that a crisis in health care existed. Most Missourians blamed the crisis on cost shifting, malpractice claims, the high cost of advanced technology and competition among hospitals, and greed among health care providers. Among Missourians there was no consensus on how to reduce these escalating costs. There was consensus that all Americans should have access to health care, but not on how to pay for these services. People were evenly divided about whether they would be willing to pay more taxes to fund universal coverage, and there was little support for passing legislation requiring individuals to carry health insurance. There was general support for insurance reform. Although consensus was not apparent in the focus groups, several common themes emerged; these themes reflected the competing models championed at the federal level. Potential solutions offered during the focus groups included the following: implementation of cost controls, increased use of nurses and physician assistants, enactment of tort reform, easing of restrictions on equity-sharing and risk-sharing ventures between hospitals and physicians, and reductions in costs created by unneccessary, "hassle" factors, such as the use of duplicate forms.

Problems Encountered After Introduction of H.B. 1622

From the time that H.B. 1622 was introduced, through hearings and floor debates in the House, a variety of problems were encountered. Despite efforts to educate members of the General Assembly, only a few members had extensive knowledge of health reform issues. Although there was public awareness of problems with the health care system, no clear consensus for reform existed. With little clear public support and a bill that offered virtually every opposition group something to dislike, the legislative debate regarding H.B. 1622 was characterized by competing groups who supported or opposed portions of the legislation. In a series of successive reductions, the scope of the bill was cut in an effort to find solid conceptual ground that would engender more support. Eventually, some support was found by narrowing the bill to a series of insurance reforms (an end to banning coverage for preexisting conditions, portability, and modified community ratings) combined with some public health initiatives. Unfortunately, the effort to find common ground took too long, and the legislative session expired.

Opposition Strategies

Opponents of the bill used a number of strategies to limit the development of support for the bill. Two groups, insurance agents and physicians, were highly organized, well financed, and highly effective in opposing the legislation. Their reasons for opposing the bill were largely related to the perceived impact of the bill on their areas of operation. A third group opposed to the bill was the insurance industry, which rejected any effort by the state to further regulate the control of health care insurance.

As in many states with large rural areas, insurance agents are highly effective in the political arena in Missouri. Virtually every small town has an insurance agent and these individuals are often prominent local citizens. Consequently, they often have direct access to local legislators. Knowing this, the insurance industry has created a highly effective political action program to inform insurance agents about issues that threaten them. Provisions in H.B. 1622 reduced the role of insurance agents in selling and marketing health insurance products. The insurance industry used the threatened loss of income to activate agents, but they did not attack the provisions affecting their potential loss of income. Instead, they attacked the community rating provisions. The insurance industry overstated the potential consequences of community rating to mobilize the industry. Using a recently released study of the effects of community rating in New York State, the insurance industry emphasized the worst possible outcome of community rating. This approach proved highly effective, even though the study and threat had little relevance to Missouri markets.

The media management plan anticipated this type of problem. A series of responses and information packets were developed to address this issue and the concerns about uninsured individuals. Limited state resources made it extremely difficult to respond when the insurance industry activated its highly effective fax network. With links to virtually every town in Missouri, the industry's ability to simultaneously paint a single, albeit distorted, picture of the consequences of the bill created an information management crisis that could not be overcome with the limited information resources available to the handlers of H.B. 1622.

At the same time, concerns among physicians culminated in a visit by many physicians to their representatives in the state capitol.

The physicians arrived at the capitol wearing buttons proclaiming "Patient Advocates." The visit by physicians occurred despite efforts to work with the leaders of the various state medical groups. Overall, physicians were fragmented into many small groups, each focusing on different aspects of reform.

In general, physicians were poorly informed about the effects of the bill, in part because of the complexity and the rapidity with which the process developed and in part because of their lack of information regarding health care reform. Physicians reflexively opposed the bill, despite many provisions such as the increased access provision that would have enhanced their standing. Like insurers, most small towns have physicians who are also prominent local citizens. Their opposition to the bill, in conjunction with the insurance agents, spelled doom for health care reform in Missouri.

Despite efforts to create an information base that clearly articulated the problems and several proposed solutions, the effort to pass H.B. 1622 failed in the last week in the legislative session. Although the failure of the national health reform effort has been detailed, a specific evaluation regarding the role of information and the success or failure of state health reform has not been described. The obvious causes of failure include the size of the legislative proposal and the enormity of the proposed change. The legislation would alter the flow of money and would control system resources. As occurred at the federal level, a significant amount of money promoting the status quo, combined with the simultaneous failure of national health care reform, killed reform in Missouri.

Reasons for Success of Special Interest Groups

The success of special interest groups was determined by the factors that differentiate legislative activity at the state level from that at the federal level. Included among these factors are legislators who are actively involved in another career (including officials involved in the insurance industry), limited resources for legislative staff, limited access to policy institutes and think tanks, limited availability to academic expertise, readily available national data but scarce state-level data applicable to policy analyses, limited executive branch expertise and even more limited policy analysis capacity, lobbyists' prominence and centrality to the evolution of the debate, especially given the lack of other expert resources, and limited ability to assess the impact of other state and national reform experiments on the local environment. The next section examines key aspects of the debate with reference to these points.

CASE EXAMPLES

The Uninsured

In the debate surrounding universal coverage for Missouri's uninsured citizens, questions about the cost of extending coverage to the uninsured and the accuracy of the data concerning this group overtook the dialogue. Despite data demonstrating the advantages to all Missourians of extending health insurance coverage, many concerns remained. The primary data source for the uninsured came from a 1993 commissioned report from Lewin-VHI. The report was heavily quoted during the debate. A key issue in the discussion of coverage for the uninsured was the source of funding for such an effort.

Misinformation and Lack of Information

As the issue of shifting costs to pay for the uninsured unfolded, more attention was directed to the demographics of the uninsured. During this phase of the debate, misinformation and the lack of information from Missouri were critical. Like most states (Gold et al., 1995), few data were available for Missouri citizens to guide them through the health reform debate. The Lewin-VHI report used national data sources including the Missouri subsample of the Current Population Summary (CPS). The use of the Missouri subsample of the CPS was not appreciated by most Missouri audiences. Indeed, Missouri legislators were not content to make decisions based on national data and were suspect of extrapolated census data. The staff of the ShowMe Health Reform Initiative received numerous requests to better describe how many of the uninsured could pay, how many had preexisting conditions, and a myriad of variations on these themes. Because these questions could not be answered precisely, misinformation was often substituted. As in the national debate, attributions regarding the causes of being uninsured were often invented. The lack of information about the uninsured reflected the lack of a national system to provide a comprehensive picture (Schroeder, 1996). Common examples of misinformation (see Schroeder [1996] for an excellent description of the same issues in the national debate) included allegations that a significant number of the uninsured voluntarily withdrew from the market, despite being able to participate; that most uninsured lacked coverage for only a brief period; that the uninsured received coverage anyway; and that universal coverage was too expensive.

During Missouri's health care reform debate, the small complement of legislative research staff, the absence of major academic policy consultation, and the limited availability of Missouri think tanks led to a heavy reliance on departmental (Department of Health, Department of Insurance, etc.) staff and lobbyists for professional associations. The relatively small staff of the ShowMe Health Reform Initiative was drawn from employees borrowed from the departments of Health and Insurance and the University of Missouri School of Medicine. This group was supplemented by the staff of the speaker of the House of Representatives. This small group focused on managing the process, developing legislation, and responding to input from key stakeholders. The breadth of need for education and the complexity of the issues overwhelmed the education efforts. Responding to questions from legislators during the legislative session was deemed critical, but proved difficult because of the small staff. Moreover, many of the questions required data that were not available for Missouri.

Serious questions regarding the number and characteristics of the uninsured derailed the debate (Schroeder, 1996). Because of the lack of data specific to Missouri, a campaign of misinformation from those with the greatest investment in the structure of the current health care system led to a perception that the uninsured were primarily members of a minority group, lazy, nonworking, or young and chose to be uninsured. The inability of reform advocates to carefully describe the age, sex, race, employment, and social demographics of the uninsured reduced the intensity and passion for change that this issue could have engendered. Despite public hearings that clearly documented the plight of many working Missourians, it proved as difficult in the debate at the state level as it had been in the debate at the federal level to put faces on the uninsured. Opposition from big business (Katz, 1996), especially in St. Louis, combined with opposition to other parts of the bill, overwhelmed the empathy created by the issue.

In the end, the case for covering the uninsured could not be made because of the short legislative session, the relative invisibility of the uninsured to elected officials and to the middle class, and the perception that no Missouri model existed to either count or provide health benefits for the uninsured. In addition, there was the perception that legislation expanding Medicaid passed in the previous session was sufficient to address the problem of the uninsured. When combined with the highly effective marginalization of advocates who worked for universal coverage, the debate on universal coverage was effectively halted.

Community Rating

Health insurance reform was debated throughout the legislative session and was one of the final pieces of legislation to be defeated. The final draft of H.B. 1622 included provisions for portability, guaranteed issue (requirement that health plans offer coverage to all businesses during the same period each year), and preexisting condition exclusions. Community rating was debated as a strategy to increase coverage and moderate premium increases. Community rating quickly became a battleground of misinformation. The technical elements and impacts of community rating reform could be understood by only a few people. Lobbyists became authoritative sources and the legislative leaders who were also insurance agents became the experts.

There were no neutral sources of information on this issue. Even the experience of other states became subject to interpretation. New York State's experience was persuasively described as alternately a success and a miserable failure. Insurers were said to be leaving the state in droves, and young healthy people were dropping insurance because of the soaring rates. Other states' experiences were seen as irrelevant, given the perceived uniqueness of Missouri. The complexity of the topic at both the state and national levels severely limited the ability to engage a wide audience in the debate.

Integrated Service Networks

Consolidation of hospitals into vertically integrated systems was an emerging trend during the health reform debate. Hospitals, group practices and other ambulatory services were beginning to integrate horizontally as well. These ISNs* had begun carving up the urban markets and exploring partnerships with insurance companies and seeking HMO licenses. H.B. 1622 mandated that all providers become part of an ISN in order to equitably cover the uninsured and to reduce excess system capacity, thereby driving down costs.

The market, especially in St. Louis and Kansas City, already was driving providers into networks. Throughout the rest of the state, there was remarkably little penetration by managed care. To the highly anxious physicians, the ISNs became either a form of "socialized medicine" or the "devil incarnate of managed care." The fact that few physicians in Missouri had actually been affected by changes brought about because of implementation of ISNs led to much misinformation about the potential advantages of ISNs. A proposal in the bill to create a tax on each ISN to pay for medical services for the uninsured and for public health/community health programs was ignored. This provision, if passed, would have created a significant windfall profit for physicians.

---

*At the time that H.B. 1622 was drafted, a number of names were used to describe the organization of health care systems. These systems would now be called "organized delivery systems."

In retrospect, the ISN concept was an issue that was proposed before its time: it was too complex and it was too little understood by critical groups. Although the ISN concept has subsequently proven to be the most significant market-driven reform, at the time that it was proposed it was considered a mandate from state government. Too little information on the impact on Missouri providers was made available and the issue was problematic for the remainder of the debate. Opponents saw this move as the clearest example of government-regulated health care and worried about a progression to a single-payer system.

ADDITIONAL OBSERVATIONS

Advocates of Single-Payer System

Advocates of a single-payer system found themselves in a difficult role during the debate. Having advocated for reform for years, they anticipated a bill that they would be able to support without reservation. The managed competition aspects of the bill and the lack of a single-payer mechanism created ambivalence among these advocates. They attended all of the public and legislative hearings and were actively promoting comprehensive reform. Although their "extreme" views about altering the health care system could have produced a movement toward a moderate reform package, their efforts actually undermined reform.

Opponents of H.B. 1622 characterized the sweeping reforms in the bill as preliminary steps to a single-payer system. This elicited the opposition of moderates. Advocates of a single-payer system continued to push for more comprehensive reform, but this position eventually limited their voice in the debate. This ultimately robbed the bill of the support that the single-payer advocates could have provided.

Concerns of the Middle Class

Throughout the debate, inadequate attention was given to the concerns of the middle class. In focus groups, letters to the editor, and public testimony, most middle-class citizens believed that some health care reform needed to occur, and they were easily frightened by misinformation campaigns about their own insurance rates (the community rating debate) and the security of their insurance coverage. The debate about universal coverage, as described above, quickly became focused on the poor and those not working. This focus reduced the interest of middle-class Missourians in supporting efforts to promote enhanced health care coverage. The components of the bill—including ISNs, medical malpractice reform, health care quality and information system reforms, and public health changes—meant little to most middle-class working people.

Health Reform Efforts of Other States

Other states' efforts were interpreted by advocates in a variety of ways. As stated previously, although community rating was seriously considered during the health reform debate, the experience of New York State was used alternately to promote the advantages of community rating and simultaneously to describe the outrageous rate increases and reductions in coverage likely with community rating reforms. Although significant efforts were under way in Minnesota, Washington, and Oregon, to comprehensively alter the health care system, these states were seen as, at the least, not comparable to Missouri and at the worst, "Communist reforms." There was little debate regarding governments' role in health system reform. Because of the strong leadership role of government officials in this debate, it was tempting to describe all health care reforms as government takeovers of the health care system.

Interest Groups

Many of the key interest groups (physicians, nurses, and consumers) were led by volunteers with limited knowledge of the highly technical areas of the health system and insurance reform. Often, these key interest group leaders relied on lobbyists for education on these technical issues. In this manner, lobbyists quickly occupied critical roles in the debate. Because lobbyists were known to key stakeholders prior to the inauguration of the health reform debate, the lobbyists had gained the trust of leaders in critical organizations. As is common in state legislatures, several prominent lobbyists worked with more than one group, which further enhanced their centrality to the debate. Thus, several lobbyists became central to the debate, often simultaneously serving several "masters." A consequence of this process was the creation of informal alliances aligned by the activities of the lobbyists. Most often, these alliances were difficult to discern, and often they were apparent only in retrospect.

Efforts After the Debate

Since the 1994 legislative session, the Missouri Department of Health has formed a new Bureau of Health Services Research, which has successfully obtained a grant from the Robert Wood Johnson State Health Reform Initiatives Program, and has continued the public-private dialogue regarding the state's health care system. Five health-related agencies at the state cabinet level have formed an interagency health policy group focusing on the development of health care quality indicators, consistent patient satisfaction measures, and the development of consistent public purchasing policies.

CONCLUSION

Missouri's ShowMe Health Reform Initiative demonstrated the complexity involved in changing from an incremental legislative model to a comprehensive health reform agenda in too short a time. When legislators serve on a part-time basis and have limited knowledge of health reform issues, the intricacies of comprehensive legislation offer many opportunities for the dissemination of misinformation that controls the legislative debate. In Missouri, a cadre of legislative leaders and leading state officials were well informed about health reform, but the many opponents created by comprehensive reform legislation, combined with the short legislative session, created numerous opportunities for the dispersion of misinformation and biased information that distorted the process.

The highly technical nature of health care reform legislation severely taxed the resources of the state government. This was exacerbated by the rapid move from incremental to comprehensive legislation that demanded more expert resources than most legislation. Although there were some connections to a university or medical school and its expert resources, the network was not adequate for the breadth of the legislative agenda.

States that have succeeded in comprehensive reform efforts have spent years in education and constituency building. States committed to reform have learned that it is critical to have strong partnerships with multiple constituents, adequate resources with expertise in providing real-time health policy analysis, and extensive public education efforts and that it is important to recognize the long-term nature of the health policy debate.

ACKNOWLEDGMENT

The authors gratefully acknowledge the input and ideas of Pamela R. Walker.

REFERENCES

Crittenden, R.A. 1993. Managed competition and premium caps in Washington State. Health Affairs 12:82–89.

Frank, R.G., and G.R. VandenBos. 1994. HealthCare Reform: The 1993–1994 Evolution. American Psychologist 49:851–854.

Gold, M., L. Burnbuaer, and K. Chu. 1995. How adequate are state data to support health reform or monitor health system change? Inquiry 32:468–475.

Guston, D.M., M. Jones, and L.M. Branscomb. 1996. Academe's place in the Legislatures. Chronicle of Higher Education, p. A44, May 31.

Katz, A. 1996. St. Louis, Missouri: Site Visit Report. In P.B. Ginsburg and N.J. Fasciano, Eds. The Community Snapshots Project: Capturing Health System Change. Princeton, N.J.: The Robert Wood Johnson Foundation.

Kingdon, J.W. 1984. Agendas, Alternatives and Public Policies, pp. 1–20. New York: Harper Collins.

Leichter, H.M. 1993. Minnesota: The trip from acrimony to accommodation. Health Affairs 12:48–58.

Lewin-VHI, Inc. 1993. Alternative Health Reform Initiatives: A Report for the Cost Control Committee of the Missouri ShowMe Health Reform Initiative. Fairfax, Va.: Lewin-VHI, Inc.

Schroeder, S.A. 1996. The medically uninsured—Will they always be with us? New England Journal of Medicine 334:1130–1133.

4
The Role of Graduate Medical Education Consortia in the Postregulatory Era in New York State

Benjamin K. Chu

The year 1994 saw the confluence of a multiplicity of national and regional forces in New York State which created an atmosphere that held promise for radically changing the regulatory environment in the state. Those that had long advocated for the restructuring of graduate medical education in a state where training graduate medical residents was a highly subsidized activity saw a unique opportunity for reform. It was an opportunity brought about by the legislative expiration of the state regulatory authority, the increasing penetration of managed care, and the election of a Republican governor with a decidedly market-oriented bent.

Many in New York had supported the concept of graduate medical education (GME) consortia as a better vehicle to meet overall state and regional workforce needs than relying on individual hospitals to reform the training of new physicians. As defined by the New York State Council on Graduate Medical Education (NYSCOGME), GME consortia are organizations convened around a medical school and embracing both hospital and nonhospital institutions engaged in training (New York State Council on Graduate Medical Education, 1988). The state's hospitals have opposed these changes in the past.

This paper examines the year-long process of policy debate and formulation centered around establishing GME consortia as a centerpiece for workforce planning and funding in the postregulatory era in New York State and the role of information in this reform process. In the end, information played a necessary role in framing and focusing the debate, but it was more a combination of political and financial realities that proved to be the sufficient forces to move all sides to a brave new world for health care policy in New York.

BACKGROUND

Graduate medical education has always been an essential core component of the mission of New York's academic teaching hospitals. Over the course of the past two decades, the training of resident physicians also became a staple for service delivery for virtually all institutions serving inner-city poor populations in the state. Of 230 licensed acute care hospitals in New York State, 103 participate in teaching programs. Powerful financial incentives built into the Medicare hospital payment system combined with equally powerful incentives provided by five iterations of New York State's regulated all-payer hospital reimbursement system (New York Prospective Hospital Reimbursement Methodology [NYPHRM I to V]) create compelling fiscal pressures to train as many residents as possible to maximize reimbursement and service delivery capacity, regardless of workforce policy needs. It has been estimated that Medicare provides an average of $70,000 per year per resident nationwide (Mullan et al., 1993). In New York State, GME payments from all carriers total approximately $190,000 per resident per year, with reimbursement from Medicare exceeding an average of $80,000 per resident (New York State Department of Health, 1995). It was partially this big business aspect of GME that spurred New York State teaching hospitals' opposition to proposed workforce changes under the Clinton Health Care Reform Plan. It was also one of the reasons that the senior senator from the state, Senator Daniel Patrick Moynihan, painted these proposals to change funding to academic institutions as "sins against the Holy Ghost" (U.S. Congress, 1994).

Although New York hospitals certainly have perennially played a role in derailing national workforce reform proposals, considerable concern has been building within the state over the shortsighted hospital-oriented goal of holding onto the status quo. Reform was first proposed by a statewide commission in 1986 and was later adopted by the NYSCOGME, a statewide independent body created by the legislature to advise on matters concerning resident education in the state. The state commission and the council called for the tighter linkage between educational goals and statewide workforce policy goals for residency programs through the development of GME consortia. The council defines a GME consortium as "an organization of institutions, both teaching hospital and non-hospital sites, convened around a medical school, empowered to ensure the educational integrity of training programs and to serve as a vehicle to achieve policy goals and objectives with regard to workforce reform" (New York State Commission on Graduate Medical Education, 1986; New York State Council on Graduate Medical Education, 1988). The old system of GME reimbursement to the hospitals created a near entitlement to funding that encouraged the training of too many physicians in hospital-based specialties and in hospital settings without full regard to educational content, work-force needs, and societal goals. More balanced GME consortia, it was argued, could allow local interests and constituents to shape and modify GME programs on the basis of local and regional work-force needs. Consortia could be effective in creating a better balance between primary care and specialty programs, encouraging greater training in non-hospital ambulatory sites, fostering the training of underrepresented minorities, and stimulating rational consolidation and downsizing of program numbers and size to better reflect community needs.

Before the debate described here, the success of calls for reform over the previous decade largely centered around marginal programs to boost indirect medical education funding for primary care residency programs, a loan repayment program to provide incentives for physicians to train and remain in underserved communities, and a series of state and legislative actions that provided the stimulus for the creation of six GME consortia around the state through a variety of pilot and grant programs (New York State Council on Graduate Medical Education, 1994). The most successful GME consortium in New York has been the Graduate Medical and Dental Education Consortium of Buffalo formed in 1983. In the years since its formation, it has successfully acted as the institution of record for all graduate medical programs sponsored by the nine affiliated teaching institutions of the State University of New York at Buffalo. Under an agreement with the state, the consortium's institutions have pooled GME funds to help centrally administer all residency programs and to develop programs to meet state training goals, particularly in primary care (New York State Council on Graduate Medical Education, 1991). The creation of a similar organization has been reported at the Medical College of Wisconsin (Kochar, 1996). Despite these examples and others identified in a Maine Medical Center/Association of Academic Medical Center survey in 1993 (Kelly et al., 1994), no GME consortia to date have served the wide-ranging role envisioned by NYSCOGME for rational planning and resource allocation on behalf of a range of programs sponsored by medical schools. Even without clear-cut successful models of GME consortia undertaking these expansive sets of responsibilities, the deans of the New York State medical schools had consistently endorsed the creation of consortia through its Graduate Medical Education Committee of the Associated Medical Schools of New York (Pardes, 1995, 1996).

Soon after the demise of national health reform, a series of forces began to coalesce in New York State. These forces opened the door to major reform, even in the graduate medical education arena. The election of an upstate Republican governor with firm beliefs in market principles and a decreased role of government liquefied some of the bedrock foundation for the regulatory system in New York. The governor's spending cut and tax cut agenda required significant savings from the $23 billion a year Medicaid spending bill. Significant savings were sought through an accelerated push toward Medicaid managed care. With statewide managed care penetration approaching 25 percent (Greater New York Hospital Association Subsidiaries and Affiliates, 1995) and the rush to full enrollment in Medicaid managed care, hospitals faced the loss of GME funding. Funds paid to managed care organizations in the premiums for GME are often not reflected in the negotiated per diem rates; in addition, markedly decreased in-patient days decrease the funds paid via a per diem payment system.

In this environment, hospitals sought a means to preserve nearly $3 billion in federal and state GME funds by pushing for federal and state carve-out pools devoted to GME and with monies largely passed on to hospitals in proportions roughly equal to the status quo (Greater New York Hospital Association, 1996a). However, with multiple high-profile groups including the national Council on Graduate Medical Education (1994), the Physician Payment Review Commission (1993), the Institute of Medicine (1996) and the Pew Health Professions Commission (1995), calling for fundamental restructuring of the training of the physician workforce to better reflect regional and national needs, New York hospitals faced an uphill battle in arguing to preserve the funding to train about 15,000 residents and fellows each year, many in specialties thought to be oversupplied both nationally and in the state. NYSCOGME and the state Department of Health renewed calls for reducing the number of residents trained and reallocating slots to better reflect the state-wide need to increase the number of physicians with primary care training. These policy positions were supported with data compiled by the state Department of Health by using the American Medical Association's Medical Education and Research Database, coupled with profiling information obtained from an extensive survey of New York State physicians conducted as part of the 1994 physician licensure renewal process. This analysis highlighted the extraordinary numbers of residents being trained in specialties in which a clear oversupply existed according to a host of different workforce need methodologies. The analysis also highlighted the fact that nearly half of the graduate medical residents in New York State are international medical school graduates, precisely the pool of graduate trainees singled out for reductions by these national studies (Salsberg, 1996).

A further layer of complexity in what is arguably an enormously overbedded hospital environment (Billings et al., 1996) has been the splintering of the hospital coalition along several major fault lines. The usually monolithic group of hospitals in the state began to see the hodgepodge of cross subsidization and payment add-ons for GME, uncompensated care, and other rate adjustments in a competitive light; those benefiting from the add-ons argue both for their continuation and for such add-ons to be paid through special pooled funds, whereas those that do not benefit argue for their elimination, maintaining that such payments confer undue competitive advantages to the hospitals that receive them. The Hospital Association of New York State published a set of tables establishing the winners and losers under one reform proposal (Hospital Association of New York State, 1996). Upstate hospitals, particularly those in nonteaching environments, began to see the prospect of pooled dollars flowing from upstate premiums to downstate hospitals to fund the training of unwanted doctors and the care of the uninsured; nonteaching hospitals throughout the state could see their competitive price advantage with managed care companies eroded by these subsidies; and financially stable institutions could see continued "taxation" to support financially distressed hospitals in the face of eroding margins. To further complicate the political horizons, a Republican governor was proposing radical changes in the state system of cross subsidization, and he expected support from the Republican-led state senate, the usual source of political support for the hospital lobby.

ROUND ONE: MANDATORY MEDICAID MANAGED CARE

The first health care item on the agenda for the new Governor, George Pataki, elected in 1994, was the desire to pare back Medicaid spending in the state. The chosen route was an acceleration of a process that New York began in 1991 legislation to convert its Medicaid population to managed care. At the time, a 5-year target was set to enroll 50 percent of eligible enrollees into managed care plans. The Pataki Administration's plan called for accelerating this timetable and moving toward full enrollment to shave billions of dollars from the Medicaid bill. Hospitals, on the other hand, were intent on trying to recapture money paid in the premiums to managed care companies that were invented to cover GME costs but were absent from the per diem rates negotiated by the companies for care rendered at the hospitals.

Early on, a decision was made to submit a Health Care Financing Administration waiver application under Section 1115 of the Medicaid law to develop and implement a mandatory Medicaid managed care program for New York. To facilitate the application process and to build a consensus on the waiver application, the state Department of Health convened a Medicaid Managed Care Advisory Committee in the spring of 1995. A subcommittee was convened to look at GME issues. A large proportion of the committee members were members of NYSCOGME. The subcommittee met several times over the spring and summer and issued a draft report in October 1995 calling for the establishment of discrete pools of funds to pay for "public goods." The training of graduate medical residents was considered a public good. It was a decision that would have been easy to predict given the composition of the committee. This conclusion was widely accepted by state policymakers, given the prominence that residency training played in New York State hospitals. The committee called for the highest level of funding raised over the broadest base to support GME. It was divided, however, on the mechanism for the distribution of these funds. Hospital representatives favored codifying the current system of channeling funds to hospitals engaged in training with some incentives to foster training reform, but council representatives favored distribution through consortia. A hybrid approach was also proposed. That approach would allow funding to flow through either mechanism but would tie funding to training reforms (Medicaid Managed Care Advisory Committee, 1995).

To support the debate, NYSCOGME Subcommittee on Consortia developed a consensus paper outlining its position on the value of these entities in addressing state and regional policy goals for GME. The paper outlined specific goals and objectives for training in the state and proposed a mechanism for funding GME via consortia, with financial incentives proposed to be used to help phase in this method of payment over a 4-year period (New York State Council on Graduate Medical Education, 1995).

During the time of the deliberations, a development in Rochester, New York, provided some additional impetus to those trying to counter the argument that GME consortia could not serve as a vehicle for planning and funding residency training programs. In an attempt to trim costs, Kodak decided to move its retiree health benefits business to a managed care organization that specifically excluded Strong Memorial Hospital in Rochester from its panel of hospitals. Costs were higher at Strong primarily because of add-ons to cover GME. This decision by Kodak caused such an uproar that it galvanized the University of Rochester into proposing to Kodak and the Rochester Health Commission, a business council that has traditionally been very active in fostering communitywide health planning, the creation of a GME consortium to rationally plan and distribute pooled funds for training programs. In exchange for a commitment on the part of the business community to contribute a portion of the health premium to fund GME, the University of Rochester agreed to create a consortium inclusive of all institutions engaged in training in Rochester and with representation from key community groups and businesses to plan for and fund programs. Implicit in the arrangement was the agreement to reconfigure and reduce training programs so that they correlated more closely with the needs of the Rochester community. The consortium was to encompass institutions engaged in competitive networks and would have a heavy focus on the educational integrity of the programs. The intent of the consortium was to obtain similar commitments from the state Medicaid program and the federal Medicare program to carve out and similarly fund GME through this single vehicle. The consortium was formed in the summer of 1996. Funding through the consortium is planned for the academic year beginning in July, 1997 (Cohen, J., Senior Associate Dean for Medical Education, University of Rochester School of Medicine and Dentistry, personal communication).

In the ensuing months, political jockeying to maximize the support in the state for the 1115 waiver resulted in a compromise. A GME pool was created from funds carved out of the premiums paid to managed care plans enrolling Medicaid recipients. Funds from this pool were distributed to hospitals through a system that shadowed what would have happened under the rules of the Medicaid fee-for-service system. This temporary system allowed hospitals to recover GME funds lost in caring for more than 400,000 Medicaid managed care enrollees in the state. The Department of Health guaranteed this system for a 6-month period prior to the expiration of the NYPHRM V legislation. It postponed consideration of the use of GME consortia as the vehicle for rationally planning for workforce needs and channeling GME funds until the post-NYPHRM debate.

ROUND TWO: THE GOVERNOR'S AD-HOC TASK FORCE ON NYPHRM

With the debate shifting to defining the actual system that would replace the state's highly regulated reimbursement system, the governor convened a 20-member task force under the auspices of the Commissioner of Health to advise the governor on what he should propose for the post-NYPHRM period. Representation was broader than that in the Medicaid Advisory Committee. The task force included representatives from hospitals, managed care plans, health insurers, employers, and consumers. There was no representation from the NYSCOGME or from the Associated Medical Schools of New York. The council chairman and the chief advocate of GME consortia since the 1986 state commission were invited to testify before the task force but played no formal role in the task force's deliberations. The task force issued its report in December 1995. It called for the swift movement toward a market-driven system of negotiated hospital rates. Consistent with the earlier recommendations, the task force recognized the state's obligation to continue to fund two key public goods: uncompensated care and GME. It proposed $1.2 billion to $1.5 billion in expenditures to fund uncompensated care and to provide direct and indirect support for expansion of insurance programs for the uninsured and the creation of a $675 million pool to fund GME. This represented only a portion of the existing funding for GME. It was proposed that roughly $1 billion in additional funds could be successfully obtained through negotiations with the payers. Funding for public goods was to be derived from an assessment on payers for care that had been rendered. True to the previous recommendations, the task force acknowledged the possibility of channeling GME funds through GME consortia meeting public good priority goals for training (New York State Department of Health, 1995). Although most of the main health care constituents in the state were generally supportive of the direction of the report, they were wary of the funding levels and the proposed mechanism for financing the pools. Rather than establishing a fair and broad base of financial support for funding for public goods, the payer surcharges were seen as a tax on providers. The lobbying machinery began to gear up in anticipation of the governor's formal legislative proposal.

ROUND THREE: THE GOVERNOR'S PROPOSED POST-NYPHRM LEGISLATION

Despite promises that the proposed legislation would promptly follow the task force report and the governor's campaign pledge to eliminate the perennial delays in passing the state budget, the proposed New York Health Care Reform Act of 1996 was not issued until March 20, 1996. This was 11 days before the final state budget was to be enacted by law. The legislation followed the overall thrust of the task force report but deviated in some key essential details. The act created the pools of funds for uncompensated care and GME as called for by the task force. However, the total pool proposed for GME totaled only $295 million with another $394 million promised in the Medicaid fee-for-service rates. Furthermore, the act called for 43 percent of this pool to be distributed to upstate hospitals, reflecting the approximate percentage of distribution of the payer surcharges that would fund the pool. As a result, New York City teaching programs that ordinarily receive 80 percent of the GME dollars would receive only about a third of what they would normally get in direct medical education payments. An additional surcharge of approximately 5 percent was proposed for New York City payers. These funds would supplement the payments to New York City teaching hospitals but would have seriously affected the competitive positions of these institutions. Finally, the governor proposed large financial incentives for hospitals to join a GME consortium. Hospitals could elect to remain outside a consortium and receive 100 percent of allocated funds in the first year. In the second year, this allocation would decrease to 50 percent. In the third year of the legislation, all funding would be removed unless the institution joined a qualified consortium. Each consortium would be charged with meeting a host of statewide policy objectives that would include reducing the numbers of residents, increasing the training of primary care residents, increasing the training in under-served areas, increasing the numbers of minorities in medicine, and improving the retention of graduates in New York State (Greater New York Hospital Association, 1996b).

The governor proposed markedly reduced funding levels for GME and clearly took a stand on the imbalance in the flow of funds from upstate to downstate regions. Featuring GME consortia as the preferred vehicle for reform of GME in the state was a pleasant and welcome surprise to its advocates. However, the poison pill of reduced funding and potential regional conflicts dampened the enthusiasm. The sheer volume of so many other controversial issues addressed in the legislation raised the specter that funding through consortia would become one of a host of tradable issues in the final negotiations. A wave of criticism with regard to the lack of specificity in the bill for organizations that would direct hundreds of millions of dollars of GME funds prompted the Department of Health to ask the NYSCOGME to develop more detailed guidelines for consortia. The council responded with a second position paper outlining what it thought were the key essential ingredients for a successful consortium and setting forth a process for certification and clear outcomes measures consistent with overall state workforce goals (New York State Council on Graduate Medical Education, 1996). These guidelines were largely incorporated into the New York Senate version of the post-NYPHRM legislation with the concurrence of the Department of Health and the governor's office.

INTO THE SAUSAGE MAKER

The stage was set for a grueling debate on a crucial reform of the regulatory health care environment in New York State. However, the health care reform issue was only one of a host of major reform issues being proposed as part of the debate over the state budget. Health care reform, welfare reform, proposed changes in the workman's compensation system, school reform, and a bevy of other high-profile issues shared the limelight in this debate. Within the health care reform debate, the move to negotiated rates, funding for public goods, reform of the method of funding uncompensated care, continued support of 20 New York City-based financially distressed hospitals, equity issues between upstate and downstate hospitals, competitive issues surrounding pooled resources for GME and uncompensated care, and a myriad of health care initiatives to encourage expansion of insurance for the uninsured were among the host of issues crowding the discussion of the use of consortia to channel dedicated monies for GME. With a long history of contentious debates and late budgets, this was not going to be a smooth process. The entire legislature was up for reelection that year, creating an environment that warned lawmakers to take clear stock before making radical changes in the system.

The budget battles proved to be every bit as controversial and cantankerous as promised. Moving toward a market-oriented system with the swirl of change sweeping the country heightened the sense of competition among the stakeholders. The usual monolithic hospital lobby showed many fault lines at several crucial junctures but survived the ensuing quakes. An upstate coalition of nonteaching hospitals argued against any pooled funding for teaching and uncompensated care. Financially solvent maverick elements within the hospital lobby attempted to splinter into a group calling itself the Coalition for Fair Funding to lobby against cross subsidies for financially distressed hospitals and those serving disproportionately higher volumes of uninsured individuals. Teaching hospitals and medical schools were unified in trying to obtain maximum funding for GME but were deeply divided on the incentives to channel funds through GME consortia. The Department of Health, supported by NYSCOGME, took a strong position in support of consortia as the strongest vehicle for fostering change in training programs. The department, with the support of the state Senate, first proposed differential payments to teaching programs participating in consortia and then an incentive pool that could be distributed to hospitals or consortia at the commissioner's discretion to support statewide goals. The hospital lobby opposed any system of financial incentives to join consortia. It called for only voluntary participation. Uncharacteristically, the hospital lobby's main champion in this debate was the democratic State Assembly, whose primary thrust was counter to many of the reform proposals offered by the governor. In the past, the Republican-controlled state Senate was the body more likely to carry water for the hospitals.

The pitched battles and backroom trading finally resulted in a budget accord 104 days past the day it was supposed to have been enacted. The delay set a record for tardiness in the state. In the end, the New York Health Care Reform Act of 1996 was a grand set of compromises that preserved a good deal of the current system while charting new waters. By January 1997 a new system of negotiated rates would replace the old regulated system. Stable funding for uncompensated care and GME was secured through the creation of two funds with broad bases of revenue. The pool of funds for GME ended up with approximately 25 percent less money than what the current system provided. A critical dimension of the bill was the uncoupling of the funding in the next three years from the total numbers of graduate medical residents being trained. This allowed for rational decreases in training without financial penalties. Different contribution and distribution methodologies for Medicaid and non-Medicaid funds minimized the disruption in the flow of funds between upstate and downstate hospitals and between hospitals with different financial profiles. The methodology for funding uncompensated care better reflected true service to the poor. Special initiatives to expand health insurance would be funded. In the end, 10 percent of the $545 million non-Medicaid pool of funds for GME were set aside for distribution by the Commissioner of Health to consortia or teaching hospitals meeting the criteria for meeting statewide policies regarding workforce training. Overall, this represented a pool of approximately 4 percent of the total funds for GME to be used as an incentive for programs to join a GME consortium.

THE ROLE OF INFORMATION AND
LESSONS LEARNED

The attempt to reform a system of training graduate medical residents in a state with a preponderant financial stake in maintaining the status quo proved to be difficult but achievable. Attempts at reforming state policies and incentives are rendered more difficult by a federal system that heavily rewards teaching hospitals for staying the course. In the end, the inertia against change was overcome not so much by data and information pointing toward a more rational system but by huge changes in the health care marketplace, fiscal pressures on state coffers and hospital budgets, and the gathering momentum of consensus with regard to the irrational objective of training ever increasing numbers of physicians for a world that will in all likelihood require fewer.

Information that pointed toward the imbalances in the New York system of training graduate physicians had been accumulating for years. Information was necessary for change, but the coalescence of key forces over 2 years was required to successfully push for fundamental reform. First and foremost among these forces was the ascendancy of a new state leadership with a political rhetoric predisposed to challenging the precepts of the old system. A new market environment with market rules emphasizing winners and losers and competition over limited funds further undermined these precepts. This new market environment coldly called into question the time-honored value that New York State put into support for research, teaching, and education, which were considered public goods. These extolled missions, generously supported in the past, became potential liabilities in a market-driven environment with its laser focus on costs. Academic medical centers and other teaching hospitals in New York recognized these changes and were compelled to consider heretofore unacceptable options to preserve financing for core public goods. In the end, information helped to frame the debate, but political and financial forces created the environment that forced all the stakeholders to take stock of their new positions before coming to the table. Where information pointed in the direction, these forces forged a compromise that could meet many stakeholders' need for a modicum of stability in a vastly changing world.

The uncoupling of funding for GME to the numbers of graduate medical residents trained allowed the state to seek similar protections from the Medicare program to create the right environment to encourage the transition to a more rational base. The Medicare program responded by inviting the state to develop a full proposal to uncouple funding from the number of graduate medical residents with the goal of rationalizing the scope of New York State training programs (Greater New York Hospital Association, 1996c).* Although the financial incentives to participate in regional planning through consortia represent only a small portion of the total pool of funds, these incentives are sizable enough to make a difference to most institutions. It remains to be seen how successful these consortia will be in fostering cooperation among potentially competitive health care institutions.

For its part, NYSCOGME played a key role in the decidedly uphill battle to create incentives for collective planning and funding for residency programs with a medical education perspective. As a statewide body with representatives from teaching hospitals, medical schools, community health organizations, managed care organizations, and the New York State Medical Society, forging a consensus through the development of council-endorsed position papers in support of consortia carried a good deal of weight with the Department of Health and with the state Senate. Clear and reasoned testimony, correspondence, and position papers enhanced its influence as an impartial body advocating for change.

Some advocates for GME reform and for increasing the role of consortia in GME reform will be disappointed that the New York Health Care Reform Act of 1996 fell short of carving a dominant role for these organizations formed around a medical school. However, realists will recognize a significant victory for a largely un-

---

*The New York Medicare Graduate Medical Education Demonstration began on July 1, 1997, and is under the responsibility of HCFA's Office of Payment and Delivery within the Office of Research and Demonstration.

tested concept. The real test for the advocates will now be to translate the opportunity presented by the ability to channel significant funds into a workable model for rational planning.

REFERENCES

Billings, J., S. Kaplan, and T. Mijanovich. 1996. Projecting Hospital Utilization and Bed Need in New York City for the Year 2000. Health Research Program, Robert F. Wagner Graduate Program. March 18.

Council on Graduate Medical Education. 1994. Recommendations to Improve Access to Health Care through Physician Workforce Reform, Fourth Report. Washington, D.C.: U.S. Department of Health and Human Services.

Greater New York Hospital Association. 1996a. The Case for Preserving New York's Graduate Medical Education System. March 5. New York: Greater New York Hospital Association.

Greater New York Hospital Association. 1996b. Summary of Governor Pataki's proposed post-NYPHRM legislation. Memorandum. April 2. New York: Greater New York Hospital Association.

Greater New York Hospital Association. 1996c. Correspondence to the Greater New York Hospital Foundation, Inc., regarding a concept paper for a Medicare GME demonstration project to restructure the size, composition and focus of graduate medical education programs. July 1. New York: Greater New York Hospital Association.

Greater New York Hospital Association Subsidiaries and Affiliates. 1995. Annual Report and Statistics. New York: Greater New York Hospital Association Subsidiaries and Affiliates.

Hospital Association of New York State. 1996. Work Tables. New York: Hospital Association of New York State.

Institute of Medicine. 1996. The Nation's Physician Workforce: Options for Balancing Supply and Requirements. Washington, D.C.: National Academy Press.

Kelly, J. V., F. T. Larned, and H. L. Smits. 1994. Graduate medical education consortia: Expectations and experiences. Academic Medicine 69:931–942.

Kochar, M. S. 1996. A medical school-based GME consortium in Milwaukee. Academic Medicine 71:238–242.

Medicaid Managed Care Advisory Committee. 1995. Deliberations of the Graduate Medical Education Subcommittee. Considerations in Developing a Policy for the Financing of Graduate Medical Education in New York State. Draft report. October. Albany: Medicaid Managed Care Advisory Committee.

Mullan, F., M. L. Rivo, and R. M. Politzer. 1993. Doctors, dollars and determination: Making physician work-force policy. Health Affairs 12(Suppl.):138–151.

New York State Commission on Graduate Medical Education. 1986. The Report of the New York State Commission on Graduate Medical Education. February. Albany: New York State Commisssion on Graduate Medical Education.

New York State Council on Graduate Medical Education. 1988. Graduate Medical Education Consortia. First Annual Report. New York: New York State Council on Graduate Medical Education.

New York State Council on Graduate Medical Education. 1991. Graduate Medical Education Consortia. Fourth Annual Report. New York: New York State Council on Graduate Medical Education.

New York State Council on Graduate Medical Education. 1994. Graduate Medical Education Consortia. Fifth Annual Report. New York: New York State Council on Graduate Medical Education.

New York State Council on Graduate Medical Education. 1995. Graduate medical education consortia: A model for reform. Position paper. December 18. New York: New York State Council on Graduate Medical Education.

New York State Council on Graduate Medical Education. 1996. Graduate medical education consortia: Guidelines for certification. Position paper. March. New York: New York State Council on Graduate Medical Education.

New York State Department of Health. 1995. New Directions for a Healthier New York: Reform of the Health Care Financing System: Findings and Recommendations of Governor George E. Pataki's Ad Hoc Task Force on New York's Prospective Hospital Reimbursement Methodology. December. Albany: New York State Department of Health.

Pardes, H. 1995. Testimony Before the Ad Hoc Task Force on New York Prospective Hospital Reimbursement Methodology (NYPHRM). October 24.

Pardes, H. 1996. Regarding the governor's Health Care Reform Act of 1996. New York: Associated Medical Schools of New York.

Pew Health Professions Commission. 1995. Critical Challenges: Revitalizing the Health Professions for the Twenty-First Century. The Third Report of the Pew Health Professions Commission. San Francisco: Pew Health Professions Commission.

Physician Payment Review Commission. 1993. Annual Report to Congress. Washington, D.C.: Physician Payment Review Commission.

Salsberg, S. 1996. Graduate Medical Education and the Supply and Distribution of Physicians in New York State. Presentation to the New York State Council on Graduate Medical Education Plenary Meeting, New York, March 25.

U.S. Congress. 1994. Congressional Record 140(113):S11667. Washington, D.C.: U.S. Government Printing Office.

5
Information Trading, Politics, and Funding for the National Institutes of Health in the 104th Congress

David P. Stevens

Examination of the information trading that surrounded reauthorization legislation for the National Institutes of Health (NIH) in the 104th Congress provides a window on the political process that drives biomedical research funding in this era of limited federal budgets. NIH continues to be an icon of the American health care system and its research establishment. However, even NIH, an institution that has traditionally benefited from bipartisan and enthusiastic support, will have to do better at demonstrating its value, given the commercial pressures associated with the new national health care market and the political pressure to balance the federal budget.

Introduced by Senator Nancy Landon Kassebaum, the Chairman of the Senate Committee on Labor and Human Resources, S. 1897—the National Institutes of Health Revitalization Act of 1996—made its way successfully through the Senate in the closing moments of the 104th Congress. Nevertheless, it saw no activity in the House of Representatives. Crafting the law that defines NIH—the reauthorization process—has been an increasingly complex process in recent years. For more than 15 years passage of the law that reauthorizes NIH has not been achieved in the congressional session in which a reauthorization bill was introduced. Although the details may vary, it is likely that the themes that prevailed in political discussions around funding for biomedical research during the 104th Congress will predominate in the foreseeable future.

THE ENVIRONMENT FOR BIOMEDICAL RESEARCH FUNDING

NIH was founded in 1930. It moved to Bethesda, Maryland, in 1938 as extramural funding of medical research began to expand. With the onset of World War II the urgency and magnitude of the health needs of American troops gave modern biomedical research its seminal boost. NIH produced the first extramural contracts to universities, research institutions, and hospitals (Starr, 1982).

The momentum in biomedical research did not end with the war. Consistent growth of federal support for NIH continued at a remarkable pace in the half-century after the war. During that period NIH funding doubled every 5 years (Varmus, 1995).

This momentum cannot be sustained into the next century because of two pressures on research funding. First, expanding federal entitlements have reached a level that creates pressures that limit growth of the discretionary portion of the federal budget. Support for NIH is part of that discretionary budget. Second, the constant erosion of purchasing power brought about by inflation is unremitting.

Mandatory spending in the federal budget—so-called entitlements—increasingly drives the budgetary process. Entitlements constitute that portion of federal spending that obligates the payment of benefits to anyone who meets explicit eligibility requirements established by law. Examples of entitlements include Social Security, Medicare, and Medicaid. In 1995, mandatory spending constituted 65 percent of the federal budget. This left little wriggle room in the discretionary budget, which is only 17 percent of the total federal budget (Rimkunas, 1994). Unmodified, mandatory spending will increasingly encroach on domestic discretionary spending.

In addition, inflation gnaws at NIH funding. The Biomedical Research and Development Price Index (BRDPI) is the price index for biomedical research (Jones and Sanderson, 1996). It reflects the weight of the expenditures that are driven by the unique costs of biomedical research and accounts for many variables including indirect costs and the costs of high technology. It is one of the many components that define the overall inflation rate. BRDPI has always exceeded the gross domestic product (GDP), generally by a ratio approximating 3:2. This has broad political as well as policymaking implications—a kind of budgetary Hobson's choice—as research competes with elderly, disabled, and poor people for public support, to maintain steady state, biomedical research will require a persistent and disproportionate claim on federal resources.

Given the need for increasing budgetary restraint, on the one hand, and the unremitting nature of inflation, on the other, biomedical research funding was well treated by the 104th Congress. The Continuing Resolution for fiscal year 1996 allayed early concerns engendered by the budget-cutting strategies of both the Congress and the Clinton Administration. In a year that saw the government close because of the budget battle, Congress awarded NIH not only funding for the agency but a remarkable 5.7 percent increase as well.

This largesse is unlikely to be sustainable. First, political pressure to balance the budget builds considerable resistance to the reduction of funding for competing sources to provide increases for NIH. Second, many elected members who have come to be seen as stewards of NIH retired at the end of the 104th Congress. Notable among them were Senators Nancy Landon Kassebaum and Mark Hatfield. Both of these strong supporters of NIH were powerful and effective chairs of committees of jurisdiction—the Labor and Human Resources Committee and the U.S. Department of Health and Human Services (HHS) Appropriations Subcommittee, respectively. They left behind successors whose positions on funding for biomedical research were less assured.

POLICY ISSUES AND INFORMATION TRADING

Given the growing financial constraints in the broader budgetary context, the politics of biomedical research funding are shifting so that new emphases emerge. As a result, the information trading that characterized the political process surrounding S. 1897 in the 104th Congress came down to two principal sources of political tension. The first was the debate between earmarked research funding versus investigator-initiated funding. The second was the tension between proponents of clinical research versus proponents of basic research. On both issues, NIH found itself on the opposite side of well-organized and articulate advocacy groups in the research community.

Earmarked Research Funding

The taxpayer gains access to the politics of research funding by way of his or her elected member's advocacy for specific disease-focused research. Over the years, dozens of earmarks for specific research initiatives have been introduced into the laws authorizing NIH. Traditionally, this process was marked by appearances before appropriations hearings of a parade of advocates, often with diseases for which none but the cold-blooded could refuse funding. With ever more limited dollars, this has put well-intentioned members in a very difficult position. The dilemma has become compounded by increasing awareness of the chasm between good legislative intentions on the one hand and actual triumph over disease on the other. In defense of earmarked research funding, however, some have argued that, to a large extent, the aggregate research budget is but a composite of accumulated earmarks. Yesterday's war on cancer may be today's strong and well-funded National Cancer Institute.

In recent years NIH has come to resist new earmarked funding. In testimony in hearings before the Senate Labor and Human Resources Committee, NIH leadership presented arguments against new earmarks (Hall, 1996). This position was anchored in the principle that a strengthened peer-review process provides the best mechanism for the effective allocation of tight resources to biomedical research. They argued for a process whereby federal dollars flow through institutes that, in turn, parcel out the funds, on the basis of peer-review, to investigators with the most promising research ideas.

An additional concern underlying resistance to earmarked research funding reflects the expectation that, going into a future marked by severe budgetary restraint, newly authorized earmarked funding may not necessarily be matched by appropriation of adequately increased dollars. This could leave NIH with the dilemma of relatively fixed appropriation levels that are spread over an expanded array of programs provided by ambitious authorizing legislation.

S. 1897 was introduced with no disease-focused earmarks. Although dozens of advocacy groups argued strongly for their issues, only a few well-articulated proposals found their way to S. 1897 as amendments in the Labor and Human Resources Committee markup. Four well-articulated interests were successful: an initiative for Parkinson's disease research, a set-aside specifically for pediatrics research, enhanced funding for diabetes, and support for a program in pain research. During markup, committee members repeatedly expressed their ambivalence about earmarked funding. Nevertheless, all disease-specific amendments that were proposed were passed by voice vote. It is still difficult for members to say no to strategically crafted appeals for earmarked research funding.

It is informative to review the story of the Parkinson's disease initiative as an excellent example of a successfully orchestrated strategy. It also demonstrates how a compelling earmark can take on a life of its own and even help push the broader legislation along to Senate approval.

This initiative was successful, in large measure, due to the efforts of a grassroots advocacy organization, the Parkinson's Action Network, which is headed by an articulate and astute leader who herself is a person with Parkinson's disease. With vigorous support from this group, Senator Mark Hatfield introduced a bill in the Senate to establish centers for Parkinson's disease research, specially targeted grants for Parkinson's disease research, and other educational and coordinating strategies. Under this proposed legislation, the centers and special grants would be named for Morris Udall, a popular congressman whose career had been shortened by the disability of Parkinson's disease.

In hearings, representatives of NIH took the position that focused funding for Parkinson's disease, although well-intentioned, would not be as effective as broader funding for degenerative neurologic diseases. They reasoned that investigator-initiated research into the pathophysiology of degenerative diseases of the brain would be more likely to provide a high yield than a disease-focused strategy (Hall, 1996). This argument for investment in basic research was convincing to Senator Kassebaum, who was not among the 61 co-sponsors of the Udall bill. On the other hand, all but two members of the Labor and Human Resources Committee were among the co-sponsors. It came as no surprise, therefore, that a somewhat modified version of the Udall bill was added to S. 1897 as an amendment during markup.

The Parkinson's disease amendment provided momentum to the progress of S. 1897 through the Senate. Few were optimistic that this bill would pass the Congress because of several obstacles: it was reported back to the Senate late in the session, the press of appropriations legislation preoccupied the 104th Congress in its closing moments, and there was little interest in the House of Representatives for taking up the NIH bill. However, in spite of these issues, S. 1897 was moved along by several countervailing efforts. They included vigorous lobbying by the Parkinson's Action Network, the enormous appeal of the link of this issue with a popular member of Congress, and the widespread nature of Parkinson's disease among elected members and their families.

In addition to the push by Parkinson's disease advocates, there were energetic efforts by advocates from other representatives of the biomedical research community and the personal commitment of Senator Kassebaum to see the adoption of administrative efficiencies that were proposed in her bill. These all contributed to the ultimate passage of S. 1897 in the Senate by unanimous consent. In the end, the Parkinson's initiative—resisted by NIH because of its earmarking strategy—was a substantial force that, with allies, came close to ensuring the success of the larger reauthorization bill. It was all the more ironic that support for a disease-specific earmark contributed so substantially to the success of a bill that was originally crafted to free NIH from numerous legislative mandates.

Clinical versus Basic Research

Budgetary constraints and the dramatic expansion of knowledge in basic biomedical science have combined to create a heightened struggle between proponents of funding for basic and clinical research. *Basic research* is the pursuit of fundamental biomedical knowledge. *Clinical research* is patient-focused research. The latter seeks to relate basic research to patient care. The successful pursuit of basic genetic mechanisms of disease in particular has increasingly been fueled by the commitment of NIH peer-review study sections. There is the prevailing sense that this research strategy is hot on the trail of the molecular explanation of disease. As the queue for limited research dollars has lengthened because of these new and productive areas of inquiry, clinical investigators have found themselves nearer the back of the line.

The issues surrounding funding for clinical research received considerable attention in a hearing before the Senate Committee on Labor and Human Resources in May 1996. This hearing, entitled "Funding for Biomedical Research in the Era of Health Care Reform," provided many groups the opportunity to present to Congress the case that academic health centers (AHCs) are in jeopardy in the current health care environment. AHCs and their representatives argued that their academic mission—research and education in addition to patient care—made them more expensive competitors for managed care contracts. The Association of American Medical Colleges weighed in on these discussions as effective advocates for their constituents. They presented the first data regarding the threat of managed care to cross-subsidies for research from fees paid for clinical care (Cohen, 1996). Additional information came from a study performed by Lewin-VHI. That study provided compelling data regarding the potential risk to training of future clinical investigators posed for AHCs by the economic exigencies of the marketplace (Mechanic et al., 1996).

There was strong pressure from other constituencies within the academic medical community to give greater priority to clinical research. In response to this, Senator Hatfield introduced a bill that would set aside substantial funds for new grants targeted for clinical investigators. It was the result of vigorous efforts by representatives of the American Federation for Clinical Research to champion this cause. In addition, its advocates were able to muster support from more than 100 other interest groups. Ultimately, most of the components of this clinical research bill were written into S. 1897 as a result of negotiations between Senators Hatfield and Kassebaum.

NIH has attempted to accommodate these issues. The NIH director appointed an Advisory Committee on Clinical Research to explore policy options related to clinical research and other issues that surround the changes in the health care environment. The pace of their deliberations produced results too late to offset the thrust of the Hatfield Clinical Research bill (NIH Director's Panel on Clinical Research, 1996).

Should this component of the reauthorization bill survive in future versions, it is likely that further issues, including the role of health insurers in funding clinical care associated with clinical research, will find their way into these discussions.

Other Issues Surrounding Biomedical Research Funding in the 104th Congress

Information trading played a role in the 104th Congress in two other areas: the influence of small business and abortion politics, including fetal tissue research and human embryo research.

Small Business

Small business enjoyed a dominant presence in the 104th Congress. The politics of NIH funding was no exception. Under existing law, NIH and 10 other agencies must spend 2 percent of their budgets on the Small Business Innovation Research (SBIR) program. This program provides a set-aside for grants specifically based in small businesses. This proportion would increase to 2.5 percent in 1997. Many academic researchers have objected to this set-aside because of their contention that evaluation scores achieved by SBIR grants have generally been less competitive than those for proposals that come from investigators based in academic settings, RO-1 grants. John Porter, Chairman of the House DHHS Appropriations Subcommittee, sought to introduce a section into the House DHHS appropriations bill (H.R. 3755) that would require the median evaluation scores of grants made by the SBIR program to be comparable to those for proposals for RO-1 grants in similar fields. Following meetings with representatives of small business and the biotechnology industry, however, Porter withdrew his proposal.

Fetal Tissue Research and Human Embryo Research

Controversy surrounding fetal tissue research and human embryo research found little voice in the formal discussions around S. 1897. These issues that are of concern to opponents of abortion have been the source of considerable debate in previous discussions surrounding NIH funding. For example, the Continuing Resolution that funded NIH for fiscal year 1996 contained a prohibition against human embryo research. Although the possibility of prohibitions against fetal tissue research were raised in staff discussions around the Parkinson's disease research amendment to S. 1897, the issue did not materialize in the Labor and Human Resources Committee markup.

CONCLUSION

Despite an increasingly budget-driven environment and more stringent competition for a portion of the ever-smaller discretionary slice of the federal budget, NIH continues to benefit from its special favored status in Congress. Nevertheless the debate over NIH reauthorization in the 104th Congress brought to light some of the growing tensions around allocating limited dollars for competing worthy endeavors.

The debate underscored once again, how effective grassroots organizations advocating for increased funding for a special condition—in this case Parkinson's—are not only able to shape legislation through well-researched and packaged information, but are also able to be an important force in making sure that a particular piece of legislation does not get stalled as it continues to move through Congress. Such efforts are greatly helped when the advocacy campaign is linked to a well-known and well-regarded individual afflicted with the condition under consideration.

The 1995 to 1996 congressional debate over NIH reauthorization sounded a warning bell for future support of public goods such as research and teaching in a more market-oriented, competitive environment. The research mission for academic medicine going into the next century will be caught in the pincers of limited federal budgets on the one hand and the health care market's indifference on the other. Those who value biomedical research for society's or their own gain must be sensitive to the directions of this debate in Congress and will have to find a clear and compelling voice in these continuing discussions.

REFERENCES

Cohen, J. J. 1996. Statement before the Senate Committee on Labor and Human Resources, Hearing on NIH Revitalization Act of 1996 Examining Support for Biomedical Research in the Era of Health Care Reform and Budget Constraints, S. Hrg. 104-484, pp. 5–12. Washington, D.C.: U.S. Government Printing Office.

Hall, Z. 1996. Statement before the Senate Committee on Labor and Human Resources, Hearing on Reauthorization of the National Institutes of Health, Oversight Hearings on the National Institutes of Health in Preparation for the Agency's Reauthorization this Year, S. Hrg. 104-465, pp. 57–59. Washington, D.C.: U.S. Government Printing Office.

Jones, R.F., and S.C. Sanderson. 1996. Clinical revenues used to support the academic mission of medical schools, 1992–1993. Academic Medicine 71:299–307.

Mechanic, R., A. Dobson, and S. Yu. 1996. The Impact of Managed Care on Clinical Research: A Preliminary Investigation. Final report to U.S. Public Health Service. Contract No. 282-92-0041. Fairfax, Va.: Lewin-VHI, Inc.

NIH Director's Panel on Clinical Research. 1996. Progress Reports and Tenta-

tive Recommendations. Bethesda, Md.: National Institutes of Health. May
    16.
Rimkunas, R. 1994. Entitlement Spending: A Fact Sheet. Report No. 94-94 EPW.
    Washington, D.C.: Congressional Research Service.
Starr, P. 1982. The Social Transformation of American Medicine. New York:
    Basic Books.
Varmus, H. 1995. Shattuck Lecture: Biomedical research enters the steady state.
    New England Journal of Medicine 333:811–815.

6
Gene Mapping and Genetic Testing, Promises and Problems: A Case Study on an Emerging Technology

P. Pearl O'Rourke

Society is on the brink of a virtual explosion of genetic information. The discoveries are exciting not only for their scientific merit but also for the promises of improved understanding, prevention, control, and possibly, cure of human diseases. Dissecting the mysteries of the genetic code, however, raises numerous unintended legal, ethical, and social consequences that evoke issues of discrimination, confidentiality, and civil rights. The federal government has been given the formidable task of formulating policy regarding these consequences.

This paper discusses one of the first such issues brought to the U.S. Congress: health insurance discrimination based on genetic information. There is a sense of urgency on Capitol Hill to draft policy that will protect U.S. citizens from this potentially harmful consequence of genetic knowledge. This issue owes some of its prominence to the recent availability of a test for the breast cancer mutation (*BRCA1*) and the passage of the Kassebaum-Kennedy Health Insurance Reform Act of 1996 (S. 1028).

GENETIC INFORMATION AND ITS USE

The *BRCA1* test served as a wake-up call to the general public.

This highly publicized genetic diagnosis of a common disease forced the realization that everybody may be a test away from having a preexisting condition. No longer is genetic testing limited to rare diseases that affect small populations (Huntington's chorea) or diseases that affect specific racial or ethnic groups (sickle cell anemia and Tay Sachs disease). The Human Genome Project (HGP) at the National Institutes of Health (NIH) has nearly completed mapping the human genome, and almost every week another mutation linked to a type of cancer, heart disease, or other condition is identified. Investigators indicate that soon the DNA base pairs that determine an independent personality, or possibly an addiction, will be identified (Orkin and Motulsky, 1995). This new frontier of scientific knowledge has grown to a point where everyone is vulnerable.

Not only do people wonder what predictions could be made from the personal genome, but they also wonder who else will have access to the information. In this age of computers, information is a commodity. Vital statistics, be they financial, academic or health related, seem to be little more than datum points that can be entered into any number of banks. Is any of it confidential? Should it be? Who owns it? Who has the right to access it?

At the same time, the Kassebaum-Kennedy bill, which addressed the portability of insurance coverage and exclusion from coverage on the basis of preexisting conditions, focused attention on the reality of insurance discrimination. The fact that the Kassebaum-Kennedy bill specifically disallowed exclusion from coverage on the basis of genetic information highlighted the concept that genetic information may be equivalent to a preexisting condition. The possibility of stigmatization or discrimination is now a concern for the entire population.

Lobbying activity for the Kassebaum-Kennedy bill also provided numerous opportunities for the public airing of the ever powerful anecdote (Billings, 1993; Hudson et al., 1995).

- A woman who is pregnant with a child diagnosed with cystic fibrosis is told that if she carries her child to term, her insurance company will not cover any medical care that is directly related to the diagnosis of cystic fibrosis.

• A woman who has a positive test for the breast cancer gene is asked to sign a waiver on her insurance policy relieving the company of any financial responsibility to cover breast cancer-related care.

Discrimination on the basis of genetic information is not new; as early as 1975, the National Academy of Sciences issued a report on genetic screening. Commissions, boards, committees, counsels, and studies (Hanna, 1995), have also excelled at identifying and massaging the problems, but the complexity of the issues has paralyzed society into relative inaction.

Now, however, Congress cannot avoid the issue; they have been requested to confront insurance discrimination on the basis of genetic information. To understand all of the issues, members of Congress need information, they need to be educated. Numerous information brokers have volunteered to provide the information and serve as teachers. Under the guise of education, these information brokers try to influence policy. The debate of genetic information and insurance discrimination has attracted "educators" from the insurance industry, the genetic research community, the biotechnology industry, and consumer groups. None of these groups are monolithic. Each has its own agenda.

One of the items on their agenda is how to define genetic information: should this be broad and inclusive or narrow and restrictive? A broad definition includes any and all patient data that suggest a genetic condition: specific laboratory tests for chromosomes, genes, or DNA; family history; physical examination; and any laboratory test that suggests an inherited disease. For example, genetic information could be a positive test for one of the breast cancer genes (*BRCA1*), an elevated blood cholesterol level, or a family history of cystic fibrosis. In contrast, a narrow definition is limited to a specific chromosome or gene, or to DNA or laboratory tests that have been demonstrated to be valid for the diagnosis of a genetic disorder (e.g., elevated sweat chloride levels for the diagnosis of cystic fibrosis). The use of a narrow versus a broad definition of genetic information would have a significant impact on any potential policy concerning discrimination.

Physicians clearly use a broad definition of genetic information for evaluation and diagnosis. Various information brokers, however, have a vested interest in specifically promoting a broad or a narrow definition. Deciding a definition of genetic information will be an important aspect of any policy.

THE INSURANCE INDUSTRY

The private insurance industry's success depends on its ability to invest wisely and minimize financial risks. This means that it must be able to calculate the cost of coverage on the basis of the relative likelihood of the occurrence of an adverse event in an individual or a community (Hudson et al., 1995; Rothenberg, 1995; Rothstein, 1993).

Although the insurance industry represents a spectrum of insurers ranging from managed care organizations (MCOs) to the conventional insurance carrier who sells individual policies, virtually all insurers would like to participate in the process of determining policy on the use of genetic information. Few insurers, however, have volunteered any specific solutions. The topic of insurance discrimination seems to be a lose–lose proposition for the insurance industry.

MCOs as a form of community-rated health insurance will have to address genetic discrimination at two levels: entry into the plan and members' access to diagnostic and therapeutic options. Some detractors are concerned that MCOs will use genetic information to discriminate, alleging that MCOs already use marketing and enrollment practices designed to "cherry-pick" or preferentially select only low-risk health clients. Despite such allegations, at present few MCOs have specific guidelines and the MCO industry is not at the table as a unified group.

Kaiser Permanente is the exception. Its entrance policy does not allow underwriting or the use of genetic information for denying plan membership. In addition, it is developing clinical guidelines to determine which of its 6.9 million patients will have the option to receive genetic testing (Bachman and Schoen, 1996; Christensen, 1996). At present, each genetic test is considered separately, taking into account disease-specific ramifications for future health as well as proven and appropriate prevention, therapy, or cure. For example, the *BRCA1* test has serious limitations: there is a 5 to 14 percent false-positive rate, and once a mutation is identified, there are no proven methods by which to prevent the cancer from developing. Hence, *BRCA1* testing will be viewed differently than a more sensitive and specific test for a disease that can be easily and successfully treated. Kaiser Permanente's approach to the use of genetic information is commendable, but it will be an onerous, constantly evolving process that may be difficult for smaller MCOs to duplicate. Many argue, however, that market forces will force all MCOs to develop similar approaches. The consumer's decision to join a plan will be affected by the plan's policy regarding the definition and use of genetic information. Is the average consumer sophisticated enough to adequately discriminate among the different policies?

For the traditional third-party insurance carrier, some form of underwriting is the usual approach for setting premiums. Premiums are based on events and characteristics in an individual's history that may affect future health—hence, the insurance physical and laboratory examination. Most see the logic and accept setting higher premiums for people who have high-risk behaviors, such as smoking and drinking. Acceptance dwindles, however, when it is proposed that premiums be set on high-risk genetic characteristics that are totally outside a person's control. Although society has an embarrassing history of accepting discrimination on the basis of sex and race, genetic discrimination seems to have reawakened a societal concern about access to health care coverage.

What is the insurance industry's position on genetic information? A 1993 study done by the Office of Technology Assessment (OTA) reported that 75 percent of chief executive officers in the insurance industry felt that they should have the autonomy and authority to determine how to use genetic information (Office of Technology Assessment, U.S. Congress, 1992). No specific policies have been produced, however. The fact that the 1996

Kassebaum-Kennedy bill forbade the use of genetic information as a preexisting condition required the insurance industry to precipitously enter the discussion. Rather than being able to proactively introduce its policies, it was forced into a position of defense and reaction.

The insurance industry would like a very narrow or restrictive definition of genetic information. It is sensitive to the creep between DNA testing, family histories, and potentially, the routine diagnosis of a disease that has genetic implications. It would like to see genetic information limited to that derived from specific laboratory tests. Members of the industry nervously watch as various bills wend their way through the U.S. Senate and the U.S. House of Representatives, each one with seemingly more inclusive, broad definitions of genetic information. Insurers are fearful that if a broad definition of genetic information is accepted and they are not able to consider this information in determining premiums and coverage, they will be driven out of business.

One effective way that insurers have presented their concerns is by providing examples of what would happen to insurance premiums if companies were not allowed to consider any genetic data. Imagine the impact if people obtain health insurance only after they have received a genetic diagnosis that portends a significant and expensive disease. If the genetic information is confidential or cannot be considered a preexisting condition, the insurance industry's ability to accurately assess risk is destroyed and it will either lose money or have to charge everyone higher premiums.

Insurance representatives are also lobbying for uniform policies between the states. Of note, 65 percent of insurance policies fall under the Employee Retirement Income Security Act (ERISA) (Rothstein, 1993). A level national playing field is needed. To this end, insurance carriers are supplying the staffs of members of Congress with the ongoing legislative debates in each state: they emphasize the difficulties that will result from huge interstate disparities. The difficulties will be for the consumers as well as the insurance carriers.

Unfortunately, an attempt is being made to retrofit this new genetic information into the existing paradigm of insurance coverage. The insurance company is trying to perform damage control by carefully limiting and classifying genetic information. This type of solution, however, will not likely be the final one. Once the majority of people can access the information that may predict their medical future, almost everyone may have a preexisting condition that will not be covered or covered at an extraordinary cost. Can the present system of health insurance coverage meet these needs? Will the explosion of genetic information break the existing system of risk assessment and force an alternative method of providing coverage for health care?

BIOMEDICAL RESEARCHERS

The biomedical genetic research community includes basic laboratory researchers in academic and nonprofit institutions. Members of this community include HGP, the College of American Pathologists (CAP), the American Society for Human Genetics, the American College of Medical Genetics, and others (College of American Pathologists, 1996; Greely, 1995; Orkin and Motulsky, 1995). Commercial enterprises that are involved not only in research but also in the development of commercial products are categorized as the biotechnology industry.

Although the members of the research community are not monolithic in their opinions, they appreciate that the American public, which although poorly versed in the science of genetics, is fearful of the potential Big Brother mentality that could result from cataloguing genetic information. The average American citizen has been exposed to enough criminal litigation on television and in the press to recognize the concept of DNA fingerprints that can link evidence to a specific person. Such genetic paranoia could hinder or even terminate support for further research.

In response to this paranoia, the entire research community is committed to the delivery of open, truthful information to the public and, specifically, to decision makers. For many years, in an effort to build support for funding, genetic researchers marketed the promise that by unlocking genetic mysteries, diseases would be better understood, new cures would be found, and all people would live longer and healthier lives. Unfortunately, this marketing strategy created false expectations (Orkin and Motulsky, 1995). The public equated the identification of mutations with the availability of a cure. In fact, there were parents of children with known genetic diseases who decided to forego further genetic counseling or intrauterine diagnosis because "by the time my next child is born, there will be a cure." Now these same researchers are engaged in corrective advertising. They are carefully trying to educate and reeducate the public. It is clear that genetic information is becoming a household concept, and it is imperative that the research community keep the public on its side. To this end, it is piloting major public awareness campaigns. A large part of this is directed at Capitol Hill. The authorizers and the appropriators must be convinced that the information obtained by genetic research is vital and that the scientists can handle this information with appropriate caution and responsibility.

As a result, it is quite easy to attend a genetics lecture being given on Capitol Hill by none other than the director of HGP. The lectures cover basic science presented in lay language, clinical applications, promises for the future, and comments on the ethical, legal, and social implications of this material. The goal is to portray the socially responsible scientist, the available scientist. Active dialogue is a priority. The briefings have been complete and unbiased, but for audience members who had little or no prior knowledge of genetics, the briefings are more memorable for their openness and sincerity than for their specific content.

The research community is also cognizant that the information being unraveled introduces new social, ethical, and legal responsibilities and challenges (Orkin and Motulsky, 1995). In response to these concerns, HGP created the Ethical, Legal and Social Implications Program (ELSI). The charge of ELSI includes supporting and reviewing research and setting up committees or councils to address specific legal, social, or ethical issues. However, ELSI was never given the authority to set policy. Critics of this program felt that ELSI was an impotent creation and referred to it as an "unavoidable political tax," formed to appease the public and the politicians with an affirmation of social conscience (Orkin and Motulsky, 1995).

Even though ELSI does not have the mandate to form policy, the fact that there is no other policy-forming body passively empowers ELSI. People outside of HGP state that ELSI is inappropriately seen as the single "voice of the genetic research community." No single voice exists, and independent researchers as well as biotechnology industries are frustrated by this unintended power.

The lack of an authorized voice has resulted in disparate views and approaches. Several formal reports on the use of genetic information determining insurance coverage have been published. In 1993, the ELSI Task Force on Genetic Information and Insurance reported the following principles (ELSI Task Force on Genetic Information and Insurance, 1993):

1. Information about past, present, and future health, including genetic information, should not be used to deny health coverage to anyone.

2. There should be universal access to basic health services appropriate for the healthy to the seriously ill.

3. Basic health services should treat genetic diseases comparably to nongenetic diseases with appropriate testing, counseling and treatment.

4. The cost of health care should not be affected by information, including genetic information, about the past, present, or future of a person's health.

5. Access to health care should not depend on employment.

6. Access to health care should not require access to information, including genetic information, about a person's past, present, or future health care.

7. Pending universal access to basic health services, there should be alternative means of reducing the risk of genetic discrimination. Health insurers should consider a moratorium on the use of genetic tests in underwriting and insurers should undertake vigorous education efforts.

This 1993 task force report was largely ignored. The principles were simply too encompassing and the report suggested no practical solution. At about the same time, the Institute of Medicine published a report entitled *Assessing Genetic Risk* (Institute of Medicine, 1994). That report called for the following:

1. Keeping genetic testing voluntary, mandating informed consent, and keeping strict confidentiality.
2. Genetic tests must have a near zero chance for mistaken results.
3. Counseling and individual education must be available.
4. Genetic testing is human investigation until benefits and risks have been well identified and assessed.
5. Publicly supported population-based screening programs can only be justified when the disorder is of significant severity and frequency and when there are available interventions.

Then, in 1995, a workshop sponsored by ELSI and the National Action Plan on Breast Cancer proposed the following recommendations. Insurance providers should be prohibited from (Hudson et al., 1995):

1. using genetic information or the request for such to determine enrollment or coverage,
2. establishing differential rates based on genetic information or the request for genetic information,
3. requesting or requiring collection or disclosure of genetic information, and
4. releasing genetic information without written authorization for each disclosure including to whom the disclosure is being made. This prohibition includes any holder of genetic information.

All of these reports favor strong protection of the individual and any genetic information. They each recognize the implications of genetic information on access and costs of health care and they each propose very cautious approaches to the expanding use of genetic information. Part of that caution is to limit genetic testing to experimental status until more is understood about the specificity and sensitivity of specific tests as well as knowing what to do with the information. Both the Institute of Medicine and ELSI support the idea of having centralized regulation of genetic tests; this would most likely be under the auspices of the U.S. Food and Drug Administration (FDA).

In short, the information brokers that represent the full-time research community are very interested in a broad definition of genetic information. The information that they bring to the Congress is complex basic science translated for consumption by laypeople. They are very conversant in the unintended consequences of genetic information and want to proactively address these issues and be a part of the problem-solving process.

BIOTECHNOLOGY INDUSTRY

The biotechnology industry is an active participant in the genetic research community. Its distinguishing characteristic, however, is the fact that the majority of its research is directly linked to the development of a commercial product. The biotechnology industry must consider the consequences of commercialization and the need to realize a profit: this makes it difficult for members of the industry to embrace all of the propositions stated by HGP. These companies want to be able to bring their products to the marketplace as soon as it is safely possible. Any suggestion from HGP that genetic testing is experimental until benefits and risks have been well identified and assessed threatens the biotechnology industry's ability to commercialize genetic tests (Benowitz, 1996). The biotechnology industry is understandably troubled by HGP's monolithic stand on how the "research community" feels. As a result, the biotechnology industry is in the difficult position of lobbying as a research community that disagrees with HGP.

One particular area of concern is the regulation of genetic tests, possibly by FDA. This concept runs against the expressed interests of not only private industry but many of the academic research centers as well; this request for regulation is seen as HGP's attempt to destroy the competition (Benowitz, 1996). The biotechnoloy industry feels that such regulation would hurt the advancement of this science. It states that adequate regulation can be maintained by market forces as well as by existing requirements of the Clinical

Laboratories Improvement Act (CLIA). Further regulation is seen as unnecessary and counterproductive. CAP agrees with the biotechnology industry on this issue. CAP presently accredits laboratories under the auspices of CLIA and reports its findings to the Health Care Financing Administration (HCFA) (College of American Pathologists, 1996). CAP feels strongly that CLIA requirements are adequate:

> a FDA Premarket approval requirement . . . would thereby reduce the number and types of tests which are developed, reduce the number and types of commercial and academic labs that would be able to develop new tests, and delay physician and patient access to testing. . . . A better approach is to take the existing system of voluntary compliance with guidelines—a system which avoids these problems—and add to it a mechanism to ensure fuller compliance (Genzyme Corporation, 1996).

Biotechnology firms are convinced that the public will demand and should be able to obtain genetic testing as it becomes available. Market forces should be adequate to protect the quality of the available tests; federal regulation is not needed. Many have bet their financial futures on the belief that genetic research will increase the demands for genetic tests, the need for accurate tests, and the desire for genetically manipulated approaches to treatment. As a result, many of these firms are purchasing the rights to genetic processes, and they are patenting information. For example, Millennium Pharmaceuticals, Inc., in Cambridge, Massachusetts, already has $180 million in research and license agreements with three pharmaceutical firms (Johannes, 1995).

All of this information is relevant to the issue of insurance discrimination. If discrimination based on genetic information is allowed, there are a number of ways in which the biotechnology industry could be affected. Insurance companies could demand only FDA-approved laboratory tests. The insurance industry could demand tests that had been verified in clinical studies: this would relegate genetic tests to "experimental" status before these studies were completed. The term "experimental" means that the biotechnology industry would be able to charge only enough to recoup costs—a profit could not be realized. Perhaps the biggest effect would be the fact that individuals would forego genetic testing because of the fear of losing insurance coverage.

Many biotechnology firms have created their own ethics departments to better understand the evolving problems and to position themselves to be players in the resolution of these problems. OncorMed, Inc., a genetic biotechnology firm in Maryland, is providing genetic tests to institutions, but only under research protocols that are approved by an institutional review board (IRB). Because there are so many potential consumers who are not in academic centers equipped with an IRB, OncorMed has established its own IRB to review patient protocols (Hubbard and Lewontin, 1996; Murphy, 1996). By the end of 1996, OncorMed will begin marketing tests for *BRCA1* and *BRCA2* (another breast cancer mutation) and colon cancer directly to physicians—these physicians may or may not be trained in genetic counseling. Their protocols will pass through OncorMed's own IRB. Myriad Genetics in Salt Lake City, Utah, will simultaneously begin marketing clinical tests for *BRCA1*. Marketing of these tests will begin at a time when HGP has stated that testing for *BRCA1* should only be done in the confines of a research project because it is not yet known what to do with the results.

The biotechnology industry is an important player in this issue. It has been packaging its message in a number of ways. It is committed to preventing any form of discrimination on the basis of the results of genetic tests, but its message is more complex because of its desire to limit oversight and regulation of its products. Because federal regulation of these tests is a concern, the industry has been trying to demonstrate the inability of FDA to effectively approve genetic tests in a timely manner. In addition, the biotechnology industry focuses on the right of American citizens to get genetic testing if they so desire because requiring regulation and clinical testing is allowing the federal government to be too paternalistic. The industry believes that since the information is available, let individuals access it if they so desire. The present climate of antiregulation supports the concept that the government has no business regulating these products.

The biotechnology industry can effectively market itself to the disease-phobic American public simply by advertising available tests. The industry suggests that the genetic test should be seen simply as any other laboratory test; it should not be elevated to something that it is not. It supports the autonomy of the American public as well as privacy and confidentiality. In the absence of specific legislation limiting the ability to market tests, the industry is proceeding. Today in Fairfax, Virginia, Dr. Joseph Shulman will test human blood for the presence of the *BRCA1* mutation. The information belongs to the patient and to no one else. Dr. Shulman feels certain that the information is the right of the individual. But what happens when the test is positive? The false-positive rate is between 5 and 14 percent. Even if it is positive, it means that the woman has an 85 percent chance of developing breast cancer in her lifetime. Is there any way to prevent it? That is unknown. Despite the lack of information, some people are having bilateral mastectomies and oophorectomies prophylactically. Aside from the question of whether or not this is good medicine, what is the role of the insurance company? Must insurance companies be financially responsible for medical procedures that were selected on the basis of a test that the insurance company does not recognize?

CONSUMER GROUPS

A large number of consumer groups are also lobbying Congress (American Society of Clinical Oncology, 1996; Cook-Deegan, 1994; Garber and Schrag, 1996; Lerman et al., 1996). Each group, vested to its particular problem, explains how discrimination affects it now and how the expansion of genetic information threatens to make things even worse. The groups present themselves as potential victims. Virtually all of these groups express a paranoia about the potential misuses of genetic data: for example, eugenics, selective abortions, and selective sterilization. The common mantra is, "Go slowly and be careful." They are usually satisfied with ELSI's approach to the issues and appreciate the fact that HGP has focused on insurance discrimination as an important issue. The consumer groups have a shared pessimism, however, that discrimination will continue and that somehow, in some way, the insurance industry will still make the public pay.

Groups that have been victims of discrimination are concerned that genetic information will allow discriminators to better hone their actions and find new excuses for discrimination. Racial minorities have particular concern. They remember the overt insurance and employment discrimination that came with the diagnosis of the sickle cell trait in the 1970s. Sickle cell trait means that the person is a carrier of the abnormal gene, but that the person does not have the disease. Despite the fact that these people were healthy, they were denied insurance coverage and, in some cases, employment (Voelker, 1993). This unfortunately followed an already long history of racial discrimination. Although many advocacy groups for minorities plead for antidiscrimination in insurance coverage, their concerns go far beyond health insurance.

The disability advocacy groups are openly concerned about genetic cleansing. They present emotional testimony that as soon as some of these disabilities are linked to an identifiable genetic mutation, the bias will be to abort. Although they understand that some families may decide that a particular genetic burden is unfair to impose on a child, there will also be pressures of social responsibility to prevent or at least minimize the "burdens" on society. For example, consider cystic fibrosis (CF), a multisystem disease with primarily pulmonary and gastrointestinal manifestations. People with CF rarely survive beyond their 20s or early 30s. The clinical course is one of steady decline, with expensive daily medication and increasingly more frequent hospitalizations and possibly lung transplantation. The concern of disability advocacy groups is that society will say that CF is too expensive. People who carry this gene should not be allowed to conceive and bring such a child into this life to suffer and to drain society of its resources—resources that could better serve healthy children with normal projected life spans. The pressures may come from insurance, employment, and educational discrimination. These concerns are real; remember the case of the patient with CF described earlier in this paper. The disability and minority advocacy groups share the same concerns. Discrimination in providing health insurance is only a small part of the bigger picture, and this is an important battle. This is a battle of civil rights.

The disability community takes little comfort in the Americans with Disabilities Act. Title V of that act disallows discrimination only if the process of stigmatizing and selection was done with "subterfuge" in mind. This language creates a tremendous legal opportunity for health insurance discrimination (Orkin and Motulsky, 1995).

Unfortunately, few of these groups have formed any coalitions. The suggested solutions and approaches are often vague, are poorly articulated, and are tailored to primarily meet the needs of each interest group. Although most have not even considered the differences between a broad versus a narrow definition of genetic information, their presentations assume a broad definition.

Well-seasoned breast cancer advocacy groups such as the Breast Cancer Coalition have produced elegant policy statements. Its early entry into this discussion resulted from the availability and commercialization of the test for *BRCA1*. This group demands confidentiality of genetic information in its broad definition. It should be up to the woman to decide what to tell insurers, and insurers should not be able to change premiums on the basis of this information (Breast Cancer Coalition, 1996). Groups such as this that are well positioned in terms of power brokerage are the groups most likely to shape legislation.

THE U.S. CONGRESS

Congress has already taken the challenge of how to deal with genetic information in the context of discrimination. The number of briefings and hearings on HGP, genetic information, and potential discrimination attest to their commitment. Four bills in the Senate during the 104th Congress specifically addressed genetic information and discrimination: S.1416, The Genetic Privacy and Nondiscrimination Act of 1995; S.1600, The Genetic Fairness Act of 1996; S.1694, The Genetic Information Nondiscrimination in Health Insurance Act of 1996; and S. 1898, The Genetic Confidentiality and Nondiscrimination Act of 1996. The Kassebaum-Kennedy Health

Insurance Reform Act of 1996 was a fifth. The House had at least four bills: H.R. 3130, Health Coverage Availability and Affordability Act of 1996; H.R. 2690, The Genetic Privacy and Nondiscrimination Act of 1995; H.R. 2748, The Genetic Information Nondiscrimination in Health Insurance Act of 1995; and H.R. 3482, The Medical Privacy in the Age of New Technologies Act of 1996. All of these addressed similar issues, but they differed in their definition of genetic information and the way that insurance companies can handle the information. However, they all shared the goal of protecting and maintaining confidentiality.

As these bills began to emerge, a number of hearings were scheduled. Most of the witnesses provided further descriptions of the problems of discrimination and underscored the need for the federal government to provide legislation to prohibit discrimination. At present a number of states have individual laws regarding genetic information. None are identical. It is a patchwork quilt of genetic information legislation. The expansion of genetic testing, however, does not respect state borders. There must be a lead at the federal level, but there must be the certainty that the federal action does not preempt reasonable state laws.

Karen Rothenberg posed the following at a recent hearing in the Senate:

> Before we continue to expand genetic testing, how can we better quantify and qualify social risks? We must strive to resist a genetic "quick-fix" mentality that promotes genetic testing in the health care market until we have a better understanding of the risks of genetic testing. Perhaps it is even more important that we continue the public policy debate and develop the strategies to ensure that genetic information is used to benefit, not to harm, individuals and their families (Rothenberg, 1996).

Although these are desirable goals, the field of human genetics may already be too far down the road. Testing is already available for the person who is willing to pay. Genetic testing is already expanding beyond research settings in the absence of protective legislation. As genetic information continues to explode there will be numerous attempts to prohibit discrimination. However, these may be only small categorical solutions that fail to address the entire issue.

The increasing availability of genetic information will also become a factor in the health care cost debate. Genetic tests cost money. Often they must be repeated or validated by other tests. Results from genetic tests must be put into the context of a family pedigree; this requires a person trained in clinical genetics. A genetic counselor should be available to help the individual understand and digest the information. In addition, genetic diagnoses may result in new and more expensive therapies. As an extreme example: what if bone marrow transplantation became the proven therapy for persons with the genetic predisposition to a specific cancer? Bone marrow transplantation is very expensive, and in the present paradigm of financing health care, this would translate directly into an increase in health insurance premiums.

How will this play out? A most fascinating question. Although the ELSI Task Force on Insurance and Genetic Information was largely ignored, its prognostication may have been correct. Universal coverage and access to basic health care may be another one of the mysteries unlocked by the genetic revolution.

LESSONS

Educating the Member

It is important to understand how members of Congress have and continue to obtain information and advice on genetic information. Each member of Congress has a limited amount of time to invest in this technical, complex, and rapidly evolving field of science. As a result, members must rely on consultants not only to educate but also to advise. Because there are so many brokers of genetic information, members of Congress have numerous choices. Most have accessed persons or organizations that they have successfully used in the past. The result is that most members hear the information distilled by agents who know the bias of their office: that is, a member may receive all of his or her education on genetic information by the insurance trade group.

It is important to augment and fill out the potentially focused education that members may arrange for themselves. Briefings and hearings are one way to present the full story, but it is equally important for specific interest groups to visit individual offices to offer their own synopsis of the information.

The Power of the Anecdote

Anecdotes are personal, graphic, and often emotional; as such, they grab attention and demand action more quickly than does more comprehensive and broadly representative information. Although one anecdote provides interest, two anecdotes become fact. The topic of genetic information and insurance discrimination is laden with anecdotes. Although anecdotes provide illustrative examples, caution must be given whenever the lesson from an anecdote is generalized and accepted as fact.

The Temptation of Simplification

The complexity of this topic makes any potential simplification attractive. For example, rather than providing a solution for the use of all genetic information, perhaps a carve-out solution for the use of breast cancer-related genetic information would be an answer. After all, the availability of the test for the *BRCA1* mutation makes this a timely issue, the breast cancer coalition is very strong, and the women's vote is important for reelection. Similar arguments can be made for a number of specific, limited concerns, but such approaches may ultimately be destructive. A comprehensive approach is needed, not an approach that will address breast cancer mutations alone.

This is a particularly difficult problem. Unfortunately, members' enthusiasm for a cause is too often motivated by a personal interest such as a family member or a powerful group of constituents with a specific disease. It will be exceedingly important for various advocacy groups to form coalitions that can shape policy for the larger population. If every interest group tries to splinter the policy in a self-serving way, there may never be any reasonable progress.

Beware Conflicts Over Related Issues

Discussions over concerns about insurance discrimination are presently the most public arena for the discussion of genetic information. Many related concerns have been catapulted into the same arena for the purpose of gaining public awareness. One example of this is the question of regulation of genetic tests and genetic test material. While this is an extremely important issue, it is presently further complicating and confusing the discussion of genetic information and discrimination.

Members of Congress must take time to stand back and define the questions. Careful identification of the questions may prevent contamination by related but separate concerns, and it may prevent simplification of an issue that simply cannot be simplified.

REFERENCES

American Society of Clinical Oncology. 1996. Statement of the American Society of Clinical Oncology: Genetic testing for cancer susceptibility. Journal of Clinical Oncology 14:1730–1736.

Bachman, R.P., and E.J. Schoen. 1996. Managed genetic care in a large HMO. HMO Practice 10:54–58.

Benowitz, S. 1996. Scientists struggling with concerns raised by genome project progress. The Scientist 10:1–75.

Billings, P.R. 1993. Genetic discrimination. Healthcare Forum Journal. October: 35–37.

Breast Cancer Coalition. 1996. White Paper on Genetic Information. Philadelphia, Pa.: Breast Cancer Coalition.

Christensen, K. 1996. Advances In Genetic Research And Technologies: Challenges for Public Policy. Testimony of the Kaiser Permanente medical care program before the U.S. Senate Committee on Labor and Human Resources. Washington, D.C., July 25.

College of American Pathologists. 1996. Response to Federal Drug Administration's March 14, 1996 Federal Register proposal to regulate analyte reagents as Class I medical devices exempt from the premarket notification (510k) process (Docket No. 96N-0082). June 9.

Cook-Deegan, R. 1994. Private parts. The Sciences 34:18–23.

ELSI Task Force on Genetic Information and Insurance. 1993 Report. Bethesda, Md.: Ethical, Legal and Social Implications Program.

Garber, J.E., and D. Schrag. 1996. Testing for inherited cancer susceptibility. Journal of the American Medical Association 275:1928–1929.

Genzyme Corporation. 1996. A proposal for regulating predictive genetic testing. Fact Sheet. July. Cambridge, Mass.: Genzyme Corporation.

Greely, H.T. 1995. Conflicts in the biotechnology industry. Journal of Law, Medicine and Ethics 23:354–359.

Hanna, K.E. 1995. The ethical, legal and social implications program of the National Center for Human Genome Research: a missed opportunity? Pp. 432–454 *in* R.E. Bulger, E.M. Bobby, and H.V. Fineberg, eds., Society's Choices: Social and Ethical Decision Making in Biomedicine. Washington, D.C.: National Academy Press.

Hubbard, R., and R.C. Lewontin. 1996. Pitfalls of genetic testing. New England Journal of Medicine 334:1192–1194.

Hudson, K.L., K.H. Rothenberg, L.B. Andrews, M.J. Ellis Kahn, and F.S. Collins. 1995. Genetic discrimination and health insurance: An urgent need for reform. Science 270:391–393.

Institute of Medicine. 1994. Assessing Genetic Risks: Implications for Health and Social Policy. Washington, D.C.: National Academy Press.

Johannes, L. 1995. Detailed map of the genome is now ready. The Wall Street Journal, pp. B1, B11, Dec. 22.

Lerman, C., S. Narod, K. Schulman, C. Hughes, A. Gomez-Caminero, G. Bonney, K. Gold, B. Trock, D. Main, J. Lynch, C. Fulmore, C. Snyder, S. Lemon, T. Conway, P. Tonin, G. Lenoir, and H. Lynch. 1996. BRCA1 testing in families with hereditary breast-ovarian cancer. Journal of the American Medical Association 275:1885–1892.

Murphy, P.D. 1996. Testimony for OncorMed Inc. before the Senate Labor and Human Resources Committee hearing on Advances in Genetics Research and Technologies: Challenges For Public Policy. Washington, D.C., July 25.

Office of Technology Assessment, U.S. Congress. 1992. Genetic Tests and Health Insurance. Results of a Survey. Publication No. OTA-BP-BA-98. Washington, D.C.: Government Printing Office.

Orkin, S.H., and A.G. Motulsky. 1995. Report and recommendations of the panel to assess the NIH investment in research on gene therapy. December 7. Bethesda, Md.: National Institutes of Health.

Rothenberg, K.H. 1995. Genetic information and health insurance: State legislative approaches. Journal of Law, Medicine and Ethics 23:312–315.

Rothenberg, K.H. 1996. Testimony before the U.S. Senate Committee on Labor and Human Resources hearing on Advances in Genetics Research and Technologies: Challenges for Public Policy, Washington, D.C., July 25.

Rothstein, M.A. 1993. Genetics, insurance and the ethics of genetic counseling. Pp. 159–177 *in* Molecular Genetic Medicine, vol. 3. New York: Academic Press.

Voelker, R. 1993. The genetic revolution: Despite perfection of elegant techniques, ethical answers still elusive. Journal of the American Medical Association 270:2273–2274.

7
The Information Trading Process: The Case of Medicare Payment Equity

Susan Bartlett Foote

The legislative process sets the direction for health policy, but how do policymakers use information to make decisions? A better understanding of the infiormation trading process will help participants be more effective.

There are three key players in the infiormation trading process. *Information producers* include the academicians, policy analysts, researchers, and consultants who analyze data, write reports, and contribute to the knowledge base. *Information consumers* include members of the U.S. Congress and their staffs, who are the recipients of vast amounts of information.

Another key figure is the *information agent.* Some are paid by private interests, and others are paid by nonprofit public interest organizations. Often maligned as "special interests" or derided as "mere lobbyists," agents range from operators trying to sell results to those seeking to improve public policy. At their best, information agents help to define the issues, set the agenda, interpret and translate the complex and highly technical knowledge base, and respond to the needs of the legislative consumers. They can serve as conduits from producers to consumers. They can serve as catalysts to convert policy research into policy results. In the most proactive sense, these players are agents of change.

I have played all three roles in the policymaking process: as a producer of information in academia from 1980 to 1990, as a consumer during my tenure as a Robert Wood Johnson Fellow (1990 to 1991), and as a senior legislative assistant for a U.S. Senator (1991 to 1994). I am now a legislative analyst and lobbyist in the private sector. The case study presented here illustrates how an information agent can shape the policymaking process.

SUMMARY OF THE POLICY ISSUE

In 1965, Congress guaranteed health insurance coverage for retirees and disabled people. Medicare was modeled on the prevailing fee-for-service insurance programs, reflecting the way that health care was delivered at that time. Medicare paid hospitals and providers on a cost-based reimbursement system. Hospitals were paid under the Medicare Trust Fund, called Part A, and physicians were paid under Part B, which was financed through general revenues (42 U.S.C. ¶¶401–433).

In the mid 1970s, health maintenance organizations (HMOs) began to thrive in some communities as an alternative to fee-for-service. HMOs offer a comprehensive set of benefits through an organized network of providers for a single prepaid premium. In 1982, Congress gave senior citizens an opportunity to choose an alternative to fee-for-service Medicare. The HMO option, called a *risk contract*, allowed beneficiaries to select a comprehensive, integrated health plan that offered less paperwork, no deductibles, low copayments, and in many cases, more benefits than the traditional Medicare coverage (42 U.S.C. ¶¶401–433).

Congress designed a payment formula for the risk contract that was tied to fee-for-service spending. The formula requires that the Health Care Financing Administration (HCFA) total up all the fee-for-service spending in the program and calculate annually the average per capita spending (United States Per Capita Cost) and then, using the same formula, determine separate rates for each of the 3,080 counties in the nation.

Through a series of subsequent steps, HCFA derives what is known as the average adjusted per capita cost (AAPCC). The AAPCC reflects various demographic adjusters and includes Medicare Part A and Part B spending. The participating HMO risk contractors are paid 95 percent of the AAPCC.

Although the formula sounds rational in theory, in practice it has led to quite startling inequities in AAPCCs from county to county. For example, in 1995, the lowest AAPCC was $177 per beneficiary per month in Fall Rivers, South Dakota, whereas it was $647 in the Bronx, New York (Health Care Financing Administration, 1996, pp. 21–22). The primary force behind this variation is utilization patterns which are tied to the underlying capacity in the community. The work of John Wennberg at Dartmouth has demonstrated quite convincingly that the number of specialists and the number of hospital beds determines utilization in the fee-for-service system. Economists refer to this as *supply-induced demand* (Wennberg, 1996).

The formula has led to three distinct market types, two of which are characterized by below-average payment and one of which is characterized by above-average payments. The first type of market consists of rural areas, which are traditionally underserved and where fewer doctors and hospitals are readily available. Low capacity means low utilization, leading to low AAPCCs. Virtually no HMO risk plans are available in areas classified as rural. This is true even where there is HMO penetration in commercial markets in those same areas (Serrato et al., 1995).

The second type is the efficient, highly penetrated markets like Portland, Oregon; Seattle, Washington; and Minneapolis, Minnesota. Market changes have led to reductions in bed capacity per 1,000 population, more efficient use of physician resources, and price competition in the commercial side of the market. As the fee-for-service system has had to compete with managed care plans, practice styles change and utilization decreases. As a result, in these market areas the AAPCC, tied to the fee-for-service side of the ledger, is below average. In 1995, Hennepin County (Minneapolis) received $362 per beneficiary per month, and King County (Seattle) received $377—both well below the 1995 average of $400 (Health

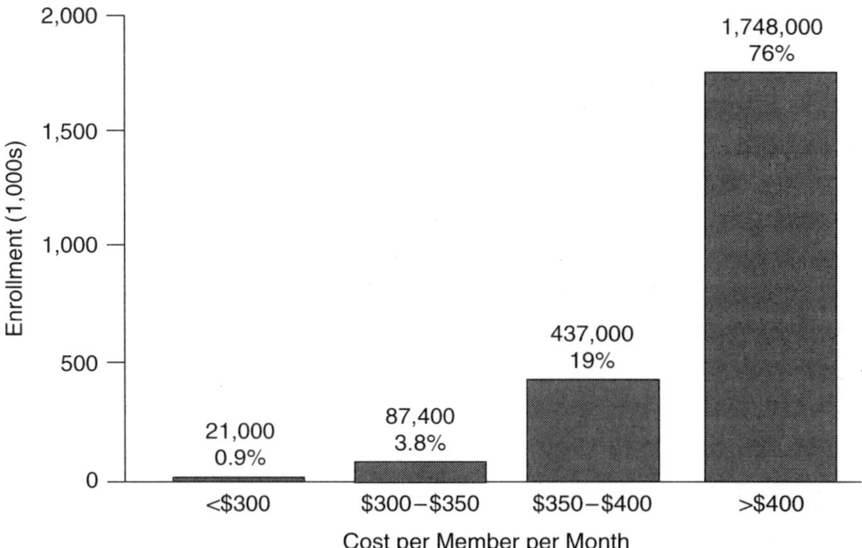

FIGURE 7.1 Medicare managed care enrollment by payment rate. SOURCE: HCFA, 1996.

Care Financing Administration, 1996, pp. 16 and 35). Figure 7.1 illustrates how risk contract enrollment reflects the payment rates available in each county.

The third type is the high-capacity markets like Miami, Florida; Philadelphia, Pennsylvania; New York, New York; and Los Angeles, California. In these markets, fee-for-service utilization is sky high, and the consequence is very high AAPCCs. The 1995 rates were $615 for Miami, $625 for Philadelphia, and $646 for New York City. (Medicare supports graduate medical education through direct and indirect spending. On average, graduate medical education [GME] was responsible for 1.8 percent of Medicare spending in 1991. New York's GME share of spending was the largest, at 3.5 percent. High GME inflates the per capita totals, raising the HMO payment [Ashby et al., 1996].)

The inequity in payment has several striking effects. Because HMOs receive 95 percent of the county AAPCC, the payment rate in some areas is much higher than the costs needed to provide the standard Medicare package. Under the Medicare program, the plans can either return the excess to the government or use it to provide additional benefits beyond those mandated in the program. In many of the markets with high payments, additional benefits now include unlimited prescription drug coverage, no additional premiums, free hearing aids, dental care, and a wide range of preventive services like exercise classes and nutrition counseling.

In efficient markets that offer HMOs, fewer additional desirable benefits are available, additional premiums are higher, and it is often a struggle for the HMO to break even. There is no incentive for health plans to enter the rural or adjacent rural markets. Figure 7.2 illustrates how resources reflect the availability of additional benefits and lower premiums.

The policy problem has several dimensions. The system is inequitable for senior citizens who have all paid in at a uniform rate during their working lives (2.9 percent of payroll earnings), because their choices and their benefits are an accident of where they happen to retire. There is also a budgetary issue, because Medicare

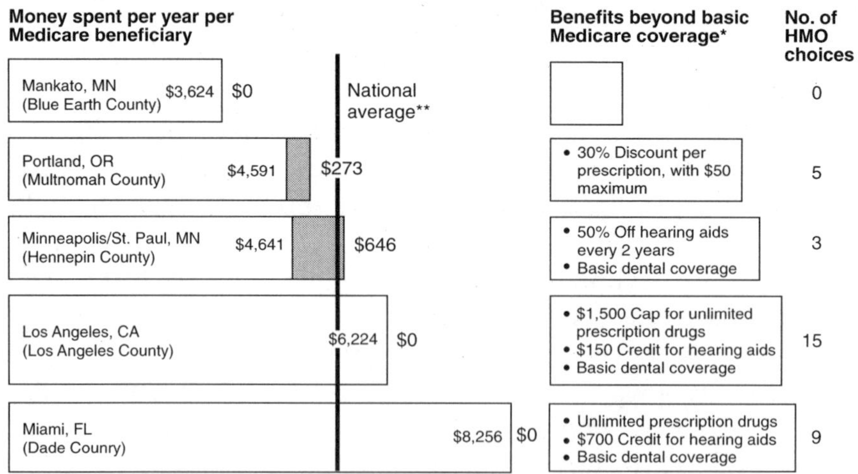

FIGURE 7.2   Benefit inequity and Medicare average adjusted per capita cost payments. *The extra benefit packages offered by HMOs often vary, even within a single county. The benefits listed here are samples of standard extra benefits available in a given county. **The vertical line denotes the national average government contribution ($40/month; $5,200/year). Open bar: government contribution; shaded bar: additional senior premium.

spending at current levels cannot be sustained within the confines of the current program (Federal Hospital Insurance Trust Fund, 1996). If Medicare reductions are necessary, how will they be made within this highly variable payment program?

SETTING THE AGENDA

The inevitability of Medicare reform hit the national stage in January 1995 following the Republican victories in the U.S. Congress in the 1994 election. The new Speaker of the House, Newt Gingrich, spoke of Medicare reform as part of a balanced budget initiative as soon as he was sworn in. He promised dramatic reductions in Medicare growth as an essential ingredient to sound fiscal budget policy (Gingrich, 1995).

A component of the Republican rhetoric was also the expansion of choices within the Medicare program. The Republican members supported moving beneficiaries into the private health plan marketplace and talked of paying a fixed amount for those plans. In the early discussions, all references to payments were based on average spending per capita. There was no mention of and little awareness of the current payment inequities on which these reforms would be overlaid.

Health plans had been living uneasily with the AAPCC formula for years. Plans in markets with low payments limited enrollment growth in some cases and held on to slim margins. The problem increased in magnitude with time, because as some markets became more efficient, they fell farther and farther below the average. Few members of Congress were aware of the problem. On the Finance Committee, Senators David Durenberger of Minnesota and Robert Packwood of Oregon had been sensitive to the issue. Durenberger had introduced a Medicare choice bill during the health reform debate of the 1993–1994 period, but the Clinton Administration had been focused on the private market, and little attention was paid to the effort (U.S. Congress, Senate, 1994).

Thus, the larger issue of Medicare reform was squarely on the agenda. The issue of inequity in payment to current risk contractors and to the alternatives promoted by Republicans was not, however.

There were a number of significant barriers to getting the inequity issue on the agenda. The first was the resistance of the national trade associations to the issue of regional inequities. Trade associations are constantly courting their members in order to enhance their power and resources in Washington, D.C. Regional inequities divide members, and most national associations try to avoid these issues at all costs.

In this case, the financial stakes were immense for some health plan interests whose growth strategies were tied to the vast revenues available in markets offering high payments (Penshorn and Johnson, 1995). The plans in these areas have considerable resources and political power. Because it is difficult to oppose equity and fairness, it served their interests to keep the issue under wraps. Their dominance in areas like California, Florida, and Texas meant that many political leaders would be pressured not to address this issue. The status quo, with double-digit increases in payments being routine, seemed too good to undo.

Finally, the complexity and technical nature of the issue made it difficult to explain. Members and staffs were overwhelmed with issues in the early months of 1995. Recall that at that time Medicare, Medicaid, tax cuts, regulatory reform, and welfare were all on the congressional plate simultaneously. In addition, there were 74 new members. Most of them had no background in Medicare policy and could not be expected to concern themselves with "details" that they could not readily understand.

OVERCOMING BARRIERS

To get the issue of Medicare payment equity on the agenda, two essential steps had to be taken. First, a base of stakeholders had to be built, and second, the story had to be told. Both steps were taken simultaneously throughout the summer and fall of 1995.

Building Stakeholders

The original stakeholders were the three risk contractors in the state of Minnesota. They included Allina Health System, Health-

Partners, and Blue Cross and Blue Shield of Minnesota. Although they are fierce competitors in the Minnesota HMO marketplace, all three agreed that the problem needed to be solved. The immediate concern was that the cuts being discussed would be imposed across the board without acknowledging the unequal payment rates. The goal was to educate members of Congress about the problem and then help shape solutions that would address the issue. The Fairness in Medicare Coalition was born.

However, Minnesota companies had trouble being heard. Their trade group, Group Health Association (recently renamed American Association of Health Plans), did not want to raise the issue directly. The Minnesota congressional delegation was not strong. The retirement of Dave Durenberger left them without a voice on the Finance Committee in the Senate. On the House side, Jim Ramstad was a new member of the Ways and Means Committee but not on the Health Subcommittee. Martin Sabo, a Democrat, had lost his seat as chairman of the Budget Committee and was now only the ranking member in a House full of partisan Republicans in the majority for the first time in decades.

Clearly, a base that included organizations from other states needed to be built. Initially, only other HMO risk contractors were approached and several from the Northwest (Oregon and Washington) were attracted to the coalition. Feelers were put out to plans in New England, Salt Lake City, and Milwaukee.

The real boost in the stakeholder base occurred when several state hospital associations saw the importance of the issue to their long-term future. Hospitals were quite concerned about the proposed reductions in the fee-for-service Medicare system, particularly in the context of growing movement toward capitated, managed care systems in the commercial markets. To compete in changing markets, many hospitals knew that they needed to be players in integrated systems of care. Access to the Medicare market is essential, especially in rural areas, where Medicare beneficiaries make up a large percentage of the population. Because the Republican plan included new choices in addition to traditional HMOs, many hospitals saw reform as an opportunity for them as well. However, the payment rate problem meant that many hospitals in states where low payments predominated knew that without AAPCC reform, the Medicare choices concept would never be a reality for them.

By the end of 1995, the Fairness in Medicare Coalition, which had begun with three Minnesota HMOs, included state hospital associations, regional hospital systems, traditional HMOs, several Blue Cross and Blue Shield plans, the Association of Family Physicians, and the Rural Referral Center Coalition. With a presence in more than 20 states as diverse as Hawaii, Maine, Iowa, and Arkansas, the coalition developed the ability to work with many members of Congress. In addition, because constituents are voters, in order for the coalition to be heard, it was much more potent to speak for constituents and to articulate why the policy issue is relevant to each member's district or state.

In this case, the role of the information agent was pivotal to the creation of the stakeholder group. Without stakeholders, there was no vehicle for policy reform, and there were no well-paved roads to bring the diverse stakeholder organizations together. The national associations were disinterested, mildly supportive, or actively hostile, and the environment pitted the hospitals against the insurers and the urban centers against the rural areas. It was crucial that the problem be clearly identified, then the organizations that would become committed to the goal could be recurited.

Developing the Message

At the same time that the base was being built, the coalition was also faced with crafting a message. There was little understanding of the issue among most of the members. Committee staffers varied in their level of interest. Some were unresponsive to the goal, for reasons that appear to be based partly on misinformation, partly because it presented another divisive issue, partly because of concern about the potentially negatively affected insurance and HMO plans in areas with high payments, and partly on policy grounds—that is, concerns about market disruption, when high payment rates would be reduced, and when low payments would be increased.

The coalition galvanized into action following a hearing in the

House Budget Committee in March, 1995. James Ehlen, the medical director at Allina Health System, was invited as a witness on HMOs in Medicare. Ehlen testified about the inequity and how it created barriers to growth of choices in the program (Ehlen, 1995). The new committee chairman, John Kasich, was intrigued. At the conclusion of the hearing, Kasich approached Ehlen and asked if Ehlen had any written material on this problem of payment inequity. The coalition had nothing to give Kasich.

The coalition set to work developing a clear statement of the problem and why it needed to be fixed. It drafted a statement of principles and a concept paper to clarify its position. The first essential task, however, was to define and describe the problem and get the issue on the table. The information producers provided plenty with which to work. There were data from HCFA, the Prospective Payment Assessment Commission, and the Prospective Payment Review Commission. John Wennberg's work provided the conceptual underpinning to the coalition's arguments.

However, the case had not been made in the political context of the U.S. Congress in a manner that would be accessible and catch the attention of the members, which is key to affecting the policy-making process. The information must be timely, accessible, and relevant to the context in which the issue is being debated. In essence, the work must be translated in order to be used.

Presented with a technically complex issue in this environment, the coalition hit upon a potent weapon—maps. The coalition developed maps of selected states, with each county color coded on the basis of its place above or below the average. The coalition started with a handful of key states and gradually invested in a complete set. The maps were a sensation. Each member saw the counties in his or her district and immediately grasped the concept of equity. Once the members were engaged, it was easier to try to explain the reasons for the problem and the implications for constituents.

Members of the coalition managed to be tapped as witnesses in the Ways and Means Committee and the Finance Committee in July 1995. The exercise of writing testimony helped refine the message and tell the story in increasingly coherent terms. The coalition worked hard to demystify the mysterious AAPCC and get to the heart of the matter. The coalition received a number of comments from staff and members who said that after reading the testimony they understood the issue of AAPCC for the first time. Being a witness gave the organization, even one as fresh to the scene as the Fairness in Medicare Coalition, visibility among the trade press and the key members of Congress.

In the fall of 1995, the coalition presented its case to the four leaders of the House Rural Health Care Caucus. Democrats included Charles Stenholm of Texas and and Glenn Pochard of Illinois and Republicans Pat Roberts of Kansas and Steve Gunderson of Wisconsin. The rural health care caucus provided the coalition with champions in the House who were willing to stand firm when the drafting process began. Although the Republicans proceeded on a fully partisan basis, members of the coalition continued to meet with rural Democrats, some of whom were working on the alternative "Blue Dog" budget bill.

On the Senate side, a meeting with Republican Senator Charles Grassley of Iowa was arranged. He immediately understood the importance of the issue to his constituents. It mattered that the Iowa Health and Hospital Systems organization was a coalition member. Once Grassley was on board, he was a tireless champion in the Finance Committee. The Finance Committee staff was accessible because the chairman, Senator Robert Packwood, understood the issue from the Oregon perspective. They knew that fair payment was a key to reforming the Medicare program.

Designing Solutions

As the drafting began and a deal was being negotiated, the coalition had to remain flexible. The process was extremely fluid as drafts and concepts were in virtual negotiation during October and November. The coalition did not want to be wedded to a single solution. There were many ways to address the problem, but specifics had to relate to the final overall Medicare reform principles. Would they choose a competitive pricing model, would they continue to administer prices tied to AAPCC with modifications, or would they decouple from the fee-for-service system? Would normalization of rates be accomplished through variable growth rate percentages or blended rates? What about graduate medical education? Indirect medical education (IME)? Disproportionate share hospital (DSH) payments?

The coalition developed a set of principles by which to measure and evaluate payment solutions. The three principles were as follows: (1) decouple the capitated payment from the fee-for-service market, (2) establish either directly or indirectly a minimum payment floor for all counties, and (3) reduce the payment variation over time and move toward a national norm. Legitimate variations based on input costs, illness, or other demographic factors could be accommodated.

As an information agent, the coalition's evaluations were provided on demand to staffers interested in protecting their boss's interests but without the technical tools to decipher proposals. When the fur began to fly, the coalition was ever present with tools for the staffers to use.

Flexibility paid off. The House and the Senate both included mechanisms to begin to resolve the inequity, but each body used very different methodologies to get there. The coalition worked closely with both bodies in an effort to ensure that the provisions were consistent with the principles, regardless of how they got there. The final bill, the Balanced Budget Act of 1995, contained all the principles that the coalition had advocated. Although the bill did not move as far or as fast as the coaltion had wanted, the coalition considered the result a major victory. The issue, unknown only months before, had a cadre of dedicated champions in both houses of Congress and was addressed in the bill.

Because the issue is regional and is based on principles, not politics, the coalition moved quickly to revive its relations with Democrats who had been sitting on the sidelines. Coalition staff worked closely with Democrats in both the House and the Senate to ensure that their alternatives also addressed the issue. Although President Clinton vetoed the Balanced Budget Act and killed the Medicare reform process for the year, his 1997 budget proposal contained all the essential elements that the coalition had advocated.

Without reform, the 1996 payment rates were implemented, further exacerbating the inequities. Figure 7.3 illustrates how the system and the potential for reform lost ground in 1996. As long as the methodology remains unchanged, there will be problems of unfairness in the program and Medicare's fiscal problems will remain unresolved.

LESSONS LEARNED

The effort described here remains a work in progress. However, some lessons can be derived from the experience to date.

First, policymaking is a process. The process takes place within a political context. The context is shaped by larger political events (like elections), ideologies, and themes that characterize and define certain periods and by personalities. Despite some earnest efforts, this is not a process that can be modeled through the use of economic assumptions, or any other assumptions for that matter. As a result, anyone who wants to participate or influence the process must have an acute sense of the context in which the issues may be raised, debated, and resolved.

Second, the three players that were identified at the outset—the producers, the consumers, and the agents—remain key. It is possible that one player can assume more than one role, but all roles are essential in the mix. For example, an agent can also be a producer, and a consumer can also be an agent. A highly informed and motivated consumer can bypass the agent and acquire knowledge directly from the producers.

How can those who are concerned about good policy outcomes (that is, legislative and regulatory outcomes that reflect a set of agreed upon principles and goals) ensure the best results possible? In my view, the outcomes are only as good as the inputs in the process. In short, gold in, gold out. Trash in, trash out. In this sense, dangers abound. Information producers must safeguard at all costs the integrity of their analyses. Some perceive the experts as being available at a price; that is, whoever buys the study buys the results. When the marketplace of ideas is dominated by the highest bidder, the process is compromised and so, too, are the results. The pro-

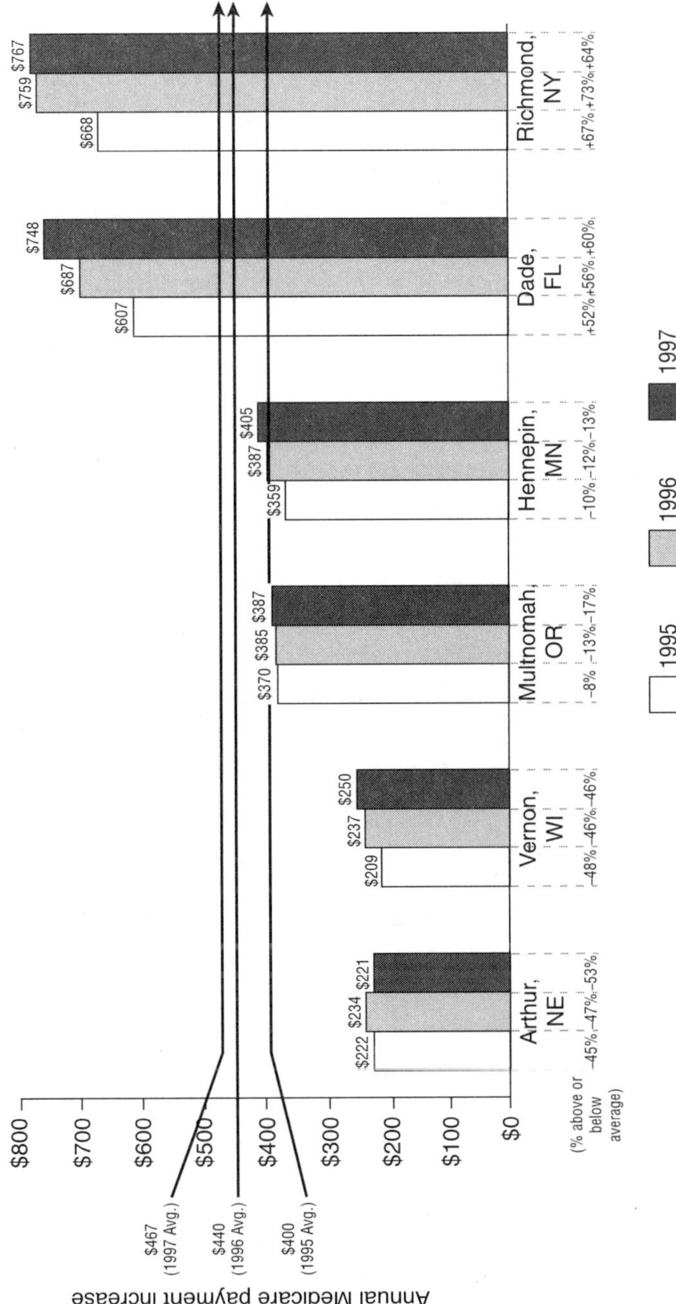

FIGURE 7.3 Annual Medicare payment increases, the gap widens. NOTE: These numbers are based on aged populations only. SOURCE: HCFA, 1996.

ducer community must protect its integrity and the public's confidence in its information.

The agents also have significant responsibilities that are honored mostly in the breach. If truth is lost in the translation, the agents subvert the infiormation trading process. When interest groups and their agents seek only short-term fixes and not improved policy outcomes, the greater good is sacrificed. When the producers allow that to occur and when the consumers passively accept the one-page quick-fix packages of some agents, everybody is a loser. This situation is exacerbated by the limited resources that now constrain the policy process.

The consumers are a constantly changing target. Elections bring new players, often with little background in public policy. The anti-incumbent, antipolitician mentality rewards candidates who have little exposure to public service or policymaking. It is hard to keep talented, well-trained, policy-oriented staff when they face low pay, long hours, and an increasingly partisan political atmosphere. This makes information consumers vulnerable to the manipulative producer and to the agents with a quick-fix message.

The experience of the Fairness in Medicare Coalition illustrates the best of the process of policymaking. The coalition's goal was first to educate and inform because it believed that an educated member would become an advocate. The coalition accurately translated data and research sources. It worked with researchers to help fill in the information gaps and to respond to research without a strong base in the literature and the data. Most importantly, the coalition articulated a set of policy principles to guide it and its supporters in the analysis of reform proposals. The coalition sought support on the basis of those principles and then worked with the experts to help design solutions that met the demands of the consumers. The coalition respected the process and its need for good, timely, and helpful information and hopes that it will ultimately prevail.

REFERENCES

Ashby, J., K. Fisher, B. Gage, S. Guterman, D. Kelley, A. Lynch, and J. Pettengill. 1996. State Variation in the Resource Costs of Treating Aged Medicare Beneficiaries. Washington, D.C.: Prospective Payment Assessment Commission.

Ehlen, J. 1995. Private Sector Solutions to Medicare. Testimony before the U.S. House Budget Committee, Washington, D.C., March 21.

Federal Hospital Insurance Trust Fund. 1996. Annual Report. Washington, D.C.: Federal Hospital Insurance Trust Fund.

Gingrich, N., 1995. All of us together must totally remake the federal government. Excerpt of speech. Washington Post, p. A12, April 8.

Health Care Financing Administration. 1996. AAPCC Ratebook. Washington, D.C.: Health Care Financing Administration.

Penshorn, J., and R. W. Johnson. 1995. The Managed Care Marketplace. Minneapolis, Minn.: Piper Jaffray.

Serrato, C., R. Brown, and J. Bergeron. 1995. Why do so few HMOs offer Medicare risk plans in rural areas? Baltimore, Md.: Health Care Financing Review 17(Fall):85–97.

U. S. Congress, Senate. 1994. Committee on Labor and Human Resources. Medicare Choice Act of 1994. S. Rept. 1996. 103d Cong., 2d sess.

Wennberg, J. 1996. The Dartmouth Atlas of Health Care. Chicago: American Hospital Publishing, Inc.

About the Authors

BENJAMIN K. CHU, M.D., M.P.H., F.A.C.P., is vice president for clinical affairs and associate dean at New York University Medical Center (NYUMC). He joined NYUMC in 1994 to help coordinate its efforts to adapt to rapid changes in the health care environment. Before coming to NYUMC, he served as senior vice president for medical and professional affairs at the New York City Health and Hospitals Corporation, and as acting commissioner of health for the City of New York. He has been active in the health reform debates on the national and local levels. He is currently a member of the New York State Council on Graduate Medical Education, serving as chair of its consortium subcommittee. He was a member of the Health Professions Review Group of the White House Task Force on Health Care Reform and was legislative assistant for health for Senator Bill Bradley (D-NJ) during his year as a Robert Wood Johnson Health Policy Fellow in 1990. Dr. Chu is a general internist by training. As a member of the Department of Medicine at the State University of New York Health Science Center at Brooklyn, he worked extensively on ambulatory care initiatives as the chief of ambulatory care and as acting director of adult emergency services. Dr. Chu received an M.P.H. from Columbia University in 1989 and an M.D. from New York University School of Medicine in 1978. He received his B.A. in 1970 from Yale University.

OLIVER FEIN, M.D., is associate dean for network affairs at Cornell University Medical College as well as an associate professor of clinical medicine and public health. As a Robert Wood Johnson Health Policy Fellow, Dr. Fein served as a legislative assistant in the office of then-Senate Majority Leader George J. Mitchell in 1994. He received a B.A. from Swarthmore College and an M.D. from Case Western Reserve University. His residency training in internal medicine was completed at Lincoln Hospital in the Bronx, an Albert Einstein College of Medicine affiliate. Subsequently, he joined the faculty at Albert Einstein College and was appointed director of Emergency Medicine at Lincoln Hospital. In 1977, he joined the Division of General Medicine at Columbia University's College of Physicians and Surgeons as director of general medicine outpatient services at Presbyterian Hospital. At Columbia Presbyterian, Dr. Fein developed the internal medicine residency ambulatory education program and initiated a faculty group practice designed to provide 24-hour-per-day/7-day-per-week physician access, continuity, and coordination of care for community patients. He also participated in building a network of four satellite community health centers in northern Manhattan. As director of Columbia University's Health of the Public Program, Dr. Fein introduced community medicine and the population perspective to dental, medical, and nursing school curricula. His research interests in health policy include urban health care delivery systems, ambulatory case mix measurement, the relationship of academic health centers to community populations and the association of social class and health status. Before his fellowship in Washington, D.C., Dr. Fein was acting director of the Division of General Internal Medicine at the Columbia Presbyterian Medical Center and associate clinical professor of medicine and public health at the College of Physicians and Surgeons of Columbia University.

SUSAN BARTLETT FOOTE, J.D., is president of Public Policy Partners, LLC, dba Durenberger/Foote. Previously, she was a professor of business and public policy in the Haas School of Business, University of California, Berkeley. She came to Washington, D.C. as a Robert Wood Johnson Health Policy Fellow in 1990, and later served as the senior health advisor to Senator David Durenberger until his retirement at the end of 1994. After leaving Capitol Hill, she became a partner in the Minneapolis-based law firm of Dorsey and Whitney and a senior vice president at APCO Associates, Inc. Ms. Foote is a widely known and respected expert on health policy. She is the author of *Managing the Medical Arms Race* and numerous other articles on medical technology policy, federal–state relations, and health reform. She is the Washington coordinator of the Coalition for Fairness in Medicare, which is seeking to reform the geographic inequities in Medicare HMO payments; she is also an officer of the Medical Technology Leadership Forum, a group of leaders in medical innovation who are seeking to educate themselves and the public on policy issues relevant to medical technology. Ms. Foote serves on the board of Lutheran Health Systems; on the Dean's Advisory Committee of the School of Public Health, University of California; and on the Public Health Trust Advisory Board. She attended Smith College and holds B.A. and M.A. degrees in history from Case Western Reserve University, and a J.D. from the University of California School of Law.

ROBERT G. FRANK, Ph.D., is professor and dean of the College of Health Professions at the University of Florida and vice president of the Rehabilitation and Behavioral Health Networks for the Shands HealthCare System. From 1991 to 1995, Dr. Frank worked on federal and state health policy. As a Robert Wood Johnson Health Policy Fellow, he worked for Senator Jeff Bingaman (D-NM). After completing the RWJ Health Policy Fellowship, Dr. Frank returned to the University of Missouri, where, as assistant to the dean for health policy, he continued to work on federal and state health policy. He also continued to work with Senator Bingaman and managed Missouri's state health reform effort, the ShowMe Health Reform Initiative. Dr. Frank has a doctorate in clinical psychology from the University of New Mexico. He is past president of the Division of Rehabilitation Psychology of the American Psychological Association and a Fellow in the Division of Rehabilitation Psychology and Health Psychology.

COLEEN KIVLAHAN, M.D., M.S.P.H., is associate chief of staff for the University Hospitals and Clinics and assistant to the dean for health policy at the University of Missouri. She is the first director of the Office of Clinical Outcomes and Medical Management. Prior to assuming this post in January 1997, she was director of the Missouri Department of Health, where she was the first woman to serve as a permanent director. After receiving her undergraduate degree from St. Louis University and her medical degree from the Medical College of Ohio at Toledo, she completed her internship and residency at the University of Missouri Medical Center. Dr. Kivlahan then became medical director at the Columbia/Boone County Health Department, where she delivered public health, primary care, and preventive services. During this period, she worked for a brief time in Washington, D.C., as medical director of the Health Resources and Services Administration, where she focused mainly on maternal and child health issues. Recognizing the need for services for the uninsured and underinsured, in 1992 she persuaded Columbia's three local hospitals and the local United Way to help set up the Boone County Family Health Center. Since the clinic's opening, Dr. Kivlahan has worked in a joint practice with other family physicians and a nurse practitioner providing primary and preventive care to low-income families.

MARION EIN LEWIN, M.A., is a senior staff officer and director of the Office of Health Policy Programs and Fellowships at the Institute of Medicine. In this position, she heads the program office for the Pew Health Policy Program, directs The Robert Wood Johnson Health Policy Fellowships Program, the IOM/American Association of Nurses Nurse-Scholar Program, and the Richard and Hinda Rosenthal Lecture Series. Ms. Lewin has been study director for several major IOM reports, including *Balancing the Scales of Opportunity: Ensuring Racial and Ethnic Diversity in the Health Professions* (1994) and *Improving the Medicare Market: Adding Choice and Protections* (1996). She currently heads an important new IOM study on "The Future of the Medical Safety Net in a New Health Care Environment." Prior to her present position, Ms. Lewin was director of the Center for Health Policy Research at the American Enterprise Institute for Public Policy Research, where she conducted research and policy studies related to the financing and delivery of health care including indigent care, Medicare and Medicaid, and private-sector health cost management efforts. Previous to this assignment she was deputy director of the National Health Policy Forum and worked as a congressional health legislative staffer. Ms. Lewin has written extensively on a wide range of health care topics, and she authors a quarterly "Washington Outlook" section for the *Journal of Medical Practice Management.* Ms. Lewin also is a contributing editor to the *Journal of the American Medical Association's* Policy Watch and a senior consultant to Grantmakers in Health. In 1996, she headed a major project for the Association for Health Services Research—the development and publication of a Baxter Health Policy Review volume called *Strategic Choices for a Changing Health Care System.* Ms. Lewin is on the Citizens Board of Providence Hospital in Washington, D.C., and chairs its Planning Committee. She received her undergraduate and graduate education at Columbia University.

P. PEARL O'ROURKE, M.D., is associate professor of anesthesia (pediatrics) at the University of Washington in Seattle and director of the Pediatric Intensive Care Unit (PICU) at the Children's Hospital and Medical Center, also in Seattle. She completed her undergraduate studies at Yale University and her medical education at Dartmouth Medical School and the University of Minnesota. Dr. O'Rourke did her internship, residency, and chief residency in pediatrics at the Massachusetts General Hospital. After a short time in primary care practice, she entered a pediatric critical care fellowship at Children's Hospital, Boston. Upon completion of the fellowship, she worked as an associate director of the Multidisciplinary Intensive Care Unit at Children's Hospital. In 1988, Dr. O'Rourke moved to Seattle, where she became director of the PICU. During her career in pediatric critical care, Dr. O'Rourke has been closely involved in the development of the extracorporeal membrane oxygenation (ECMO) program. She was a founding member of the Extracorporeal Life Support Organization, the purpose of which is to promote responsible proliferation of ECMO technology by supporting education, research, and standards. Dr. O'Rourke has also been active in the education and training of medical students, residents, and critical care fellows. In addition, she has been involved with issues in international health, having spent time in China and Indonesia. In 1996, she completed a Robert Wood Johnson Health Policy Fellowship. Dr. O'Rourke has recently accepted a position in the Office of Policy at the National Institutes of Health.

DAVID P. STEVENS, M.D., is chief academic affiliations officer for the Department of Veterans Affairs (VA), Washington, D.C. The Office of Academic Affiliations oversees formal partnerships with 105 VA-affiliated medical schools, as well as over 4,000 other universities and colleges throughout the nation. Over 34,000 medical residents, 22,000 medical students, and 45,000 associated health trainees receive a portion of their education in the VA health system every year. During the 1995–1996 academic year, he was a Robert Wood Johnson Health Policy Fellow. In this capacity he served as health policy advisor to Senator Nancy Landon Kassebaum (R-KS), who was then chair of the Senate Labor and Human Resources Committee. Prior to moving to Washington, Dr. Stevens was vice dean and Scott R. Inkley Professor of General Internal Medicine at Case Western Reserve School of Medicine. In addition to his role as vice dean, he was architect of The Robert Wood Johnson Foundation-funded Generalist Physician Initiative in collaboration with the Henry Ford Health System. A graduate of Western Reserve School of Medicine, his postgraduate studies included training at the National Institutes of Health and the Walter and Eliza Hall Institute of Medical Research in Melbourne, Australia.

WENDY B. YOUNG, R.N., Ph.D., is associate professor at the University of Illinois at Chicago (UIC) College of Nursing and faculty scholar in the UIC Great Cities Institute. As a 1995–1996 Robert Wood Johnson Health Policy Fellow, she worked on health legislation in the office of Senate Minority Leader Tom Daschle.

Since returning to UIC, she has worked on a number of projects to improve faculty and students' understanding and participation in the public policy process. Prior to her congressional fellowship, Dr. Young implemented a number of community-directed programs to demonstrate how to help local communities direct the services they recognize as essential for improving public health. One example of this is the Midwest Community Council Nursing Center, a partnership started between UIC and The Midwest Community Council, Chicago's oldest block club organization. At the center, UIC advanced practice nurse faculty provide primary care health services and health education programs. Dr. Young has studied a variety of health and health profession policy issues over the past two decades, including comparison studies of state level policy processes related to educational requirements to enter nursing practice, the nature of regulating advanced practice nurses' diagnosis and prescriptive privileges, and the patterns of nurse supply and utilization over the past decade.